So how do I say this?

If 2 (two) things are different
then there might not be any way
to _Merge_ them

Merge in that context means
bring together, make the same or similar

So once again, if there are two (2)
different, multiple things that
have a different structure

then it might not be able to combine
them together and improve one and
then eliminate the other because they
are _different_ and serve different

PURPOSES

So um, I'm the one who figured out what it was like in 1984 since thats when I was born. — I kept recreating when I came into existence through many consciousness transfers into new bodies, so I know what it was like when I came into existence and created the universe

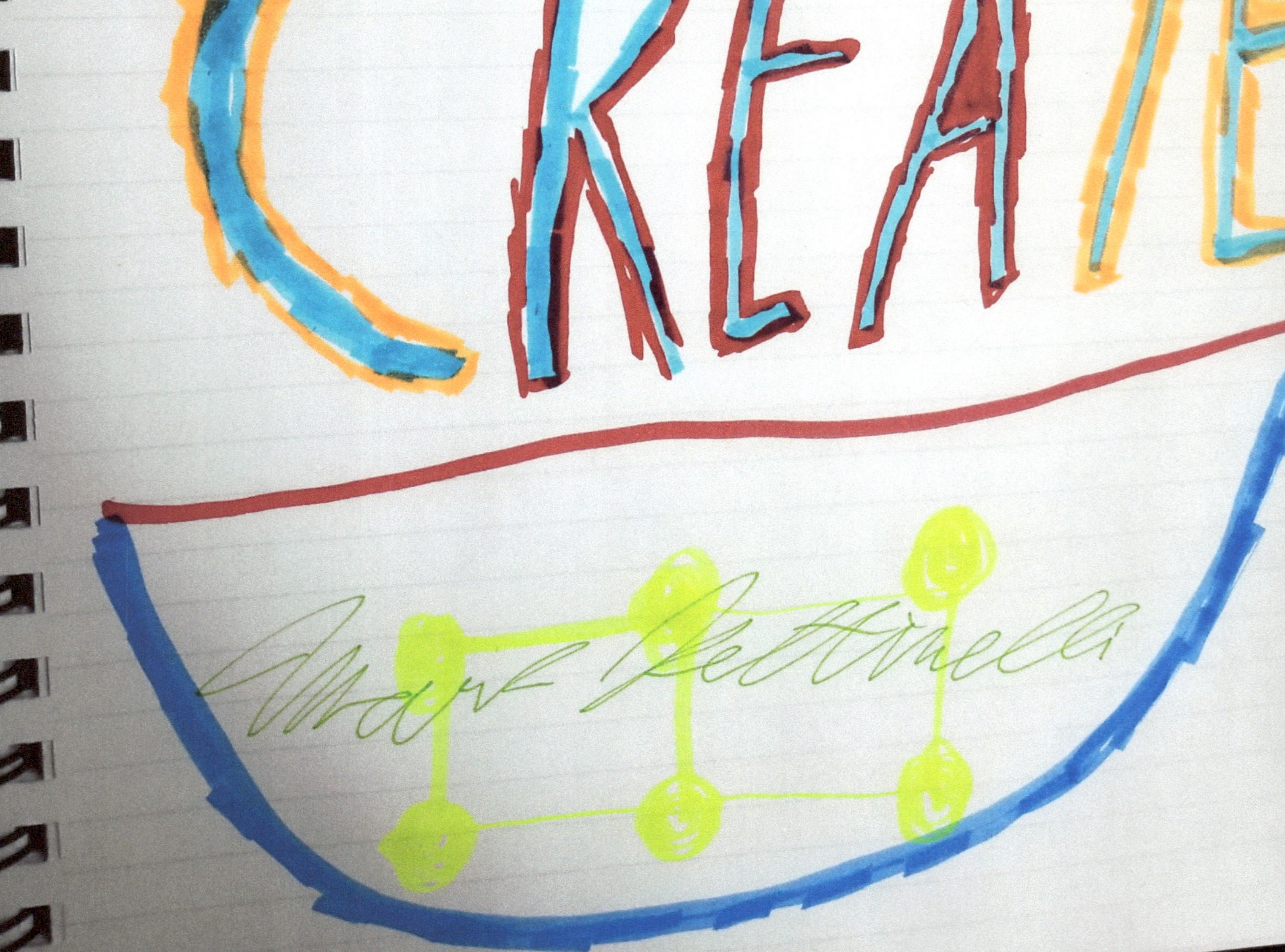

So um, I'm the one who figured out what it was like in 1984 since thats when I was born. - I kept recreating when I came into existence through many consciousness transfers into new bodies, so I know what it was like when I came into existence and created the universe

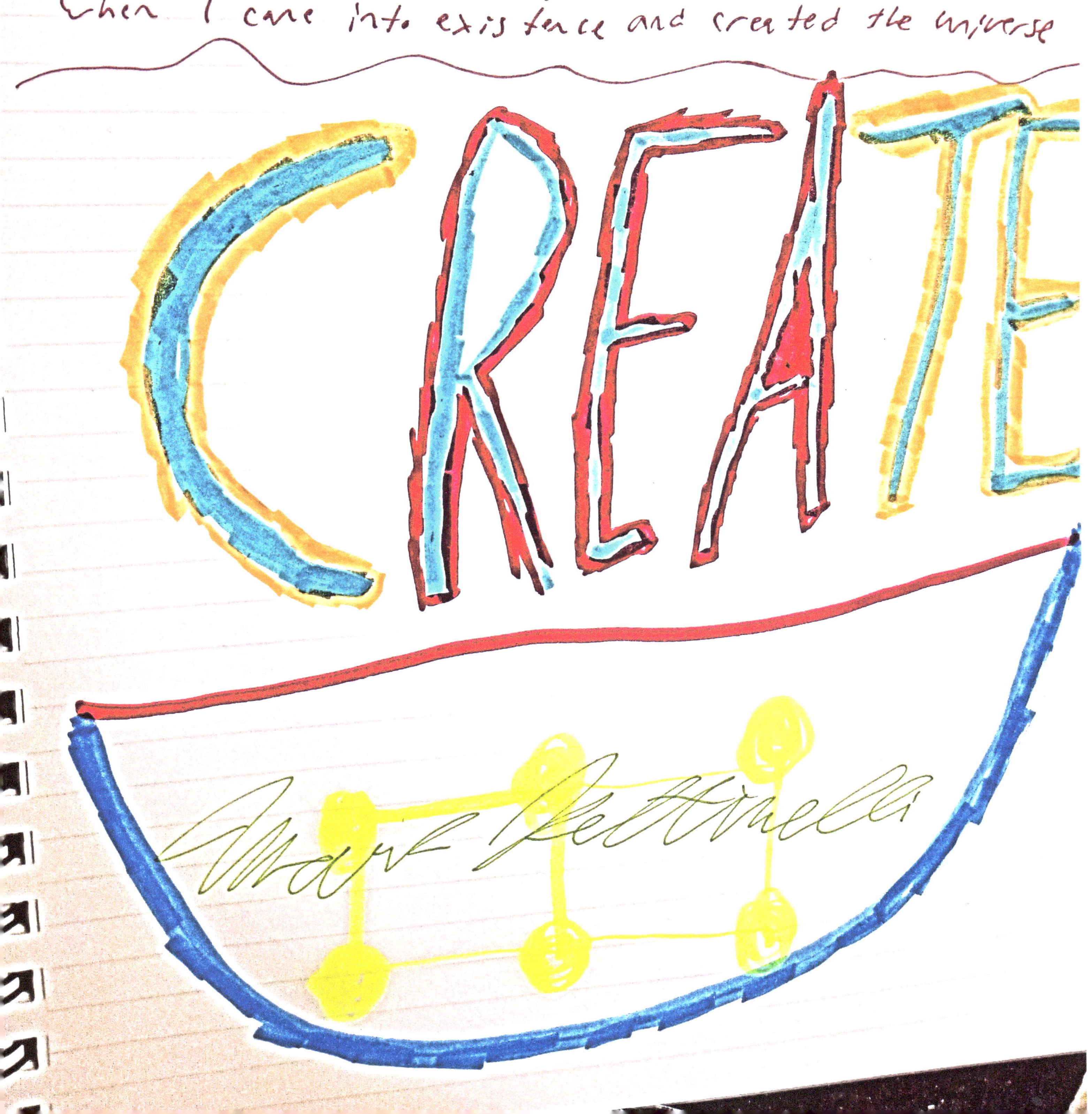

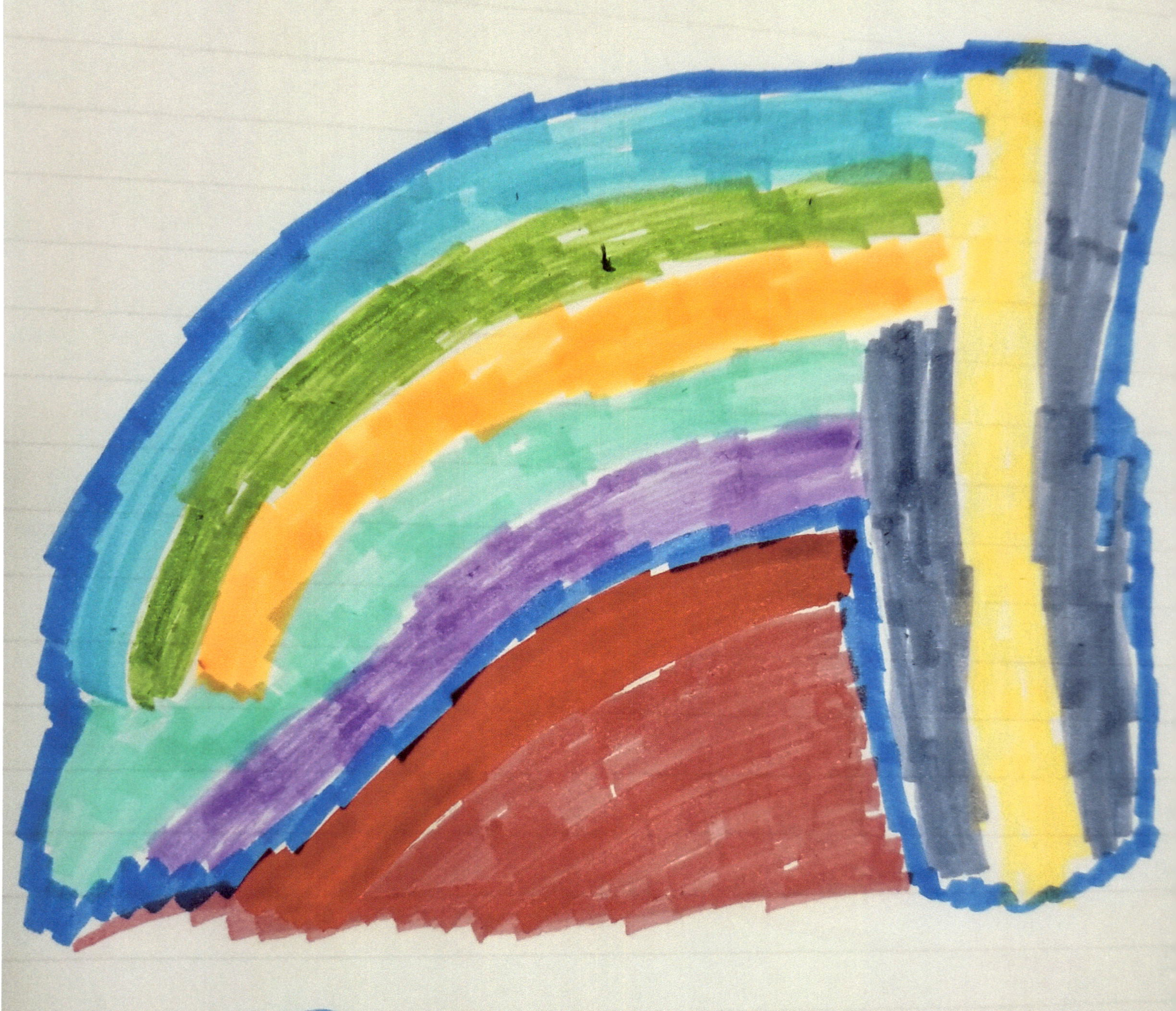

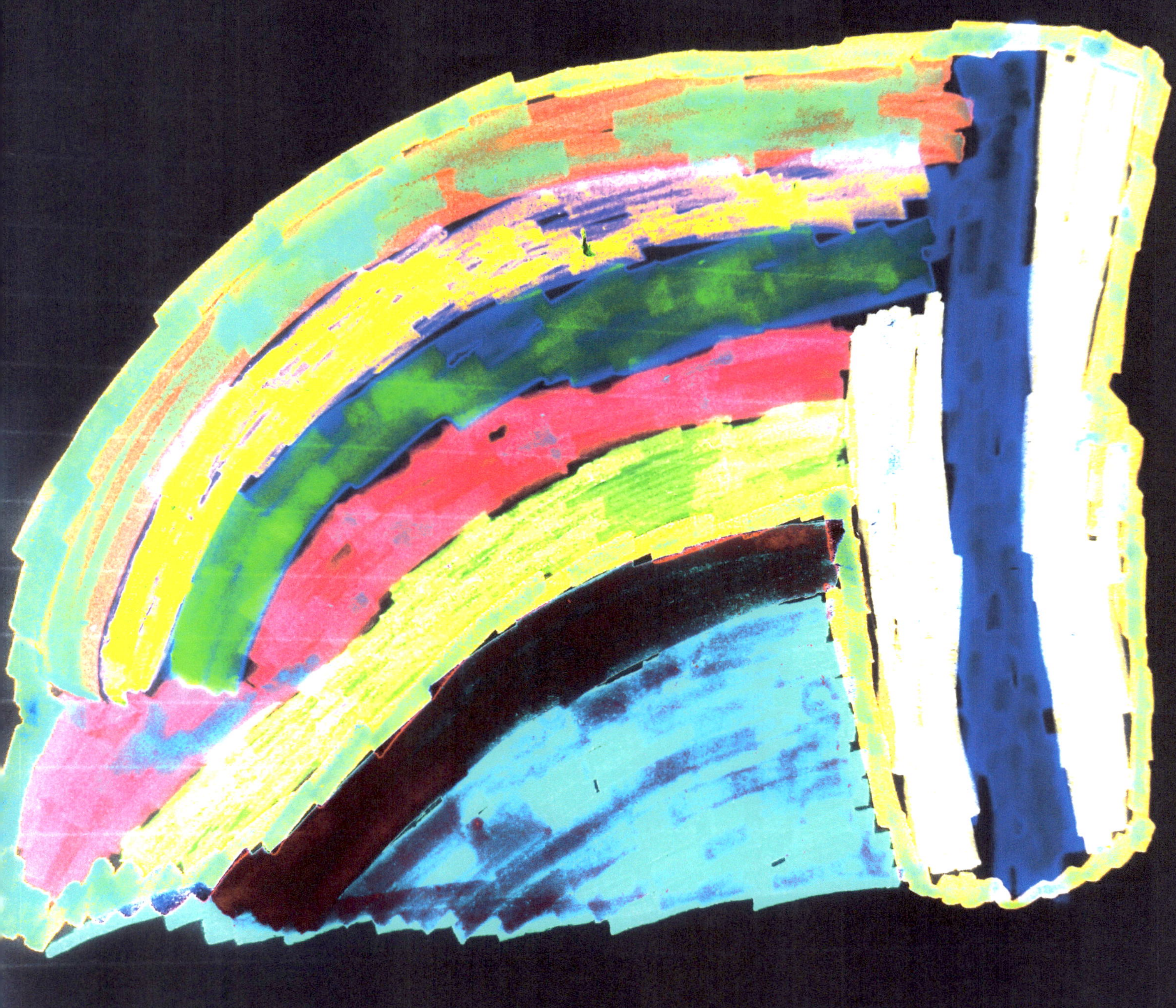

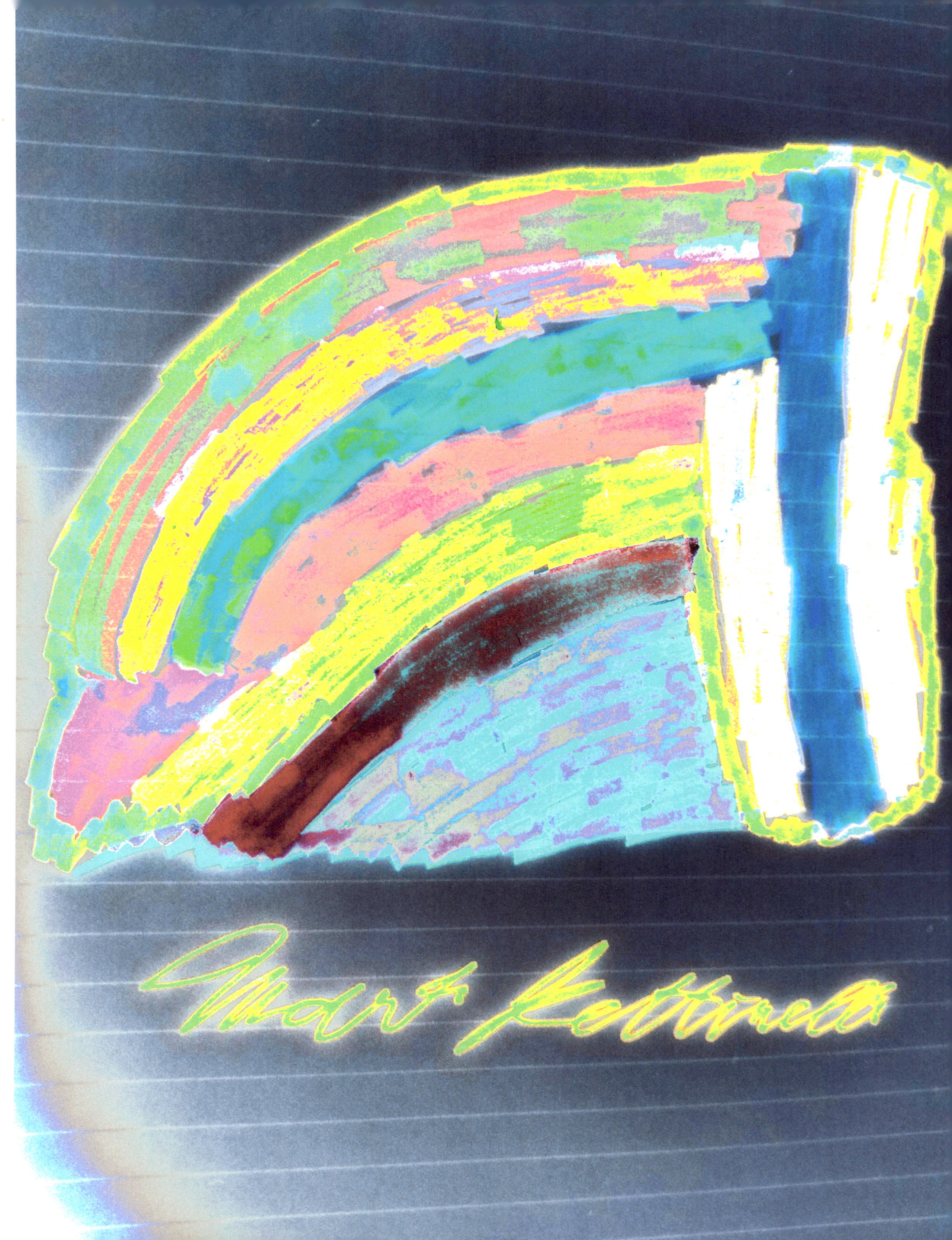
Mark Kostabi

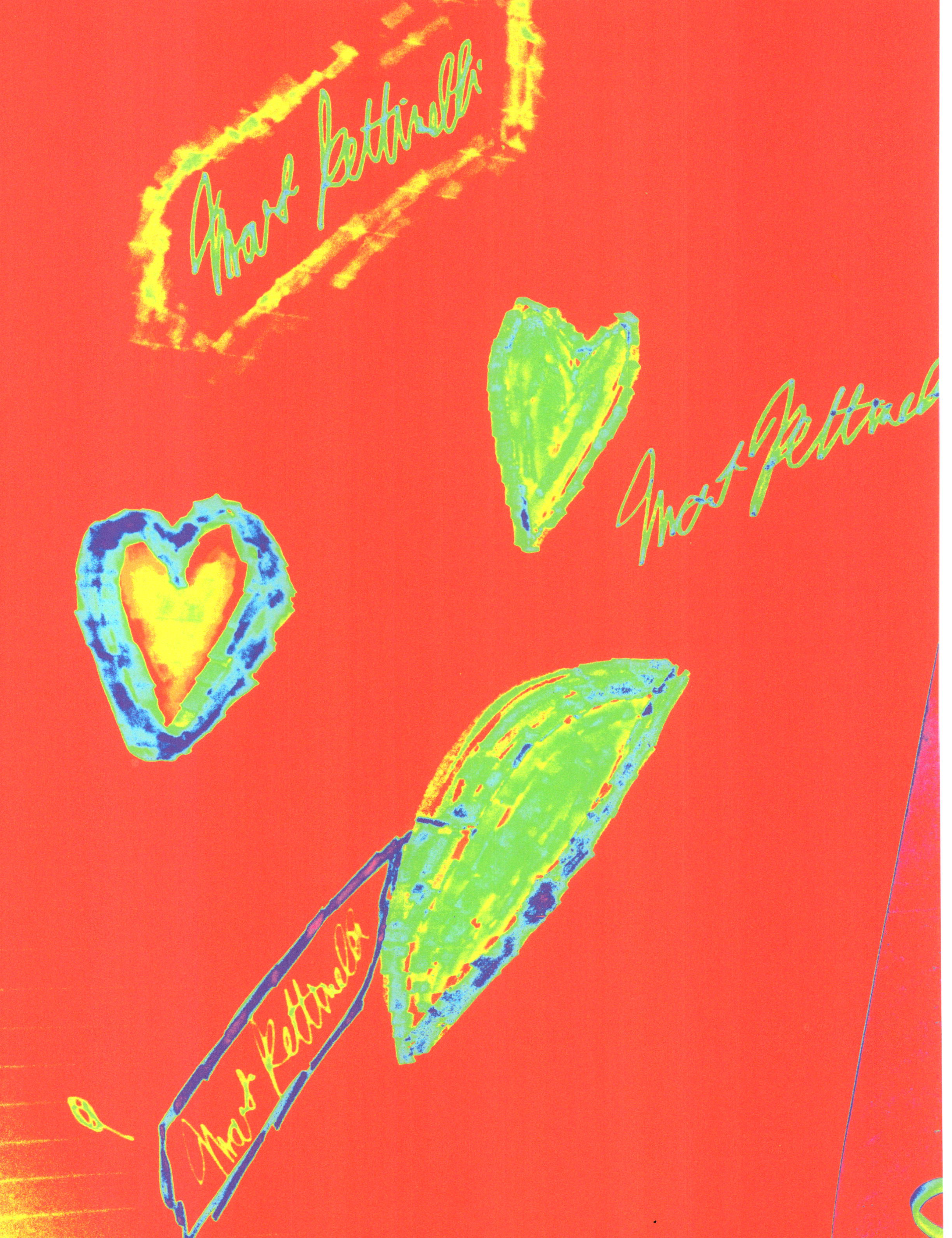

Mark Pettinelli

Mart Pettine

Mart Pettinelli

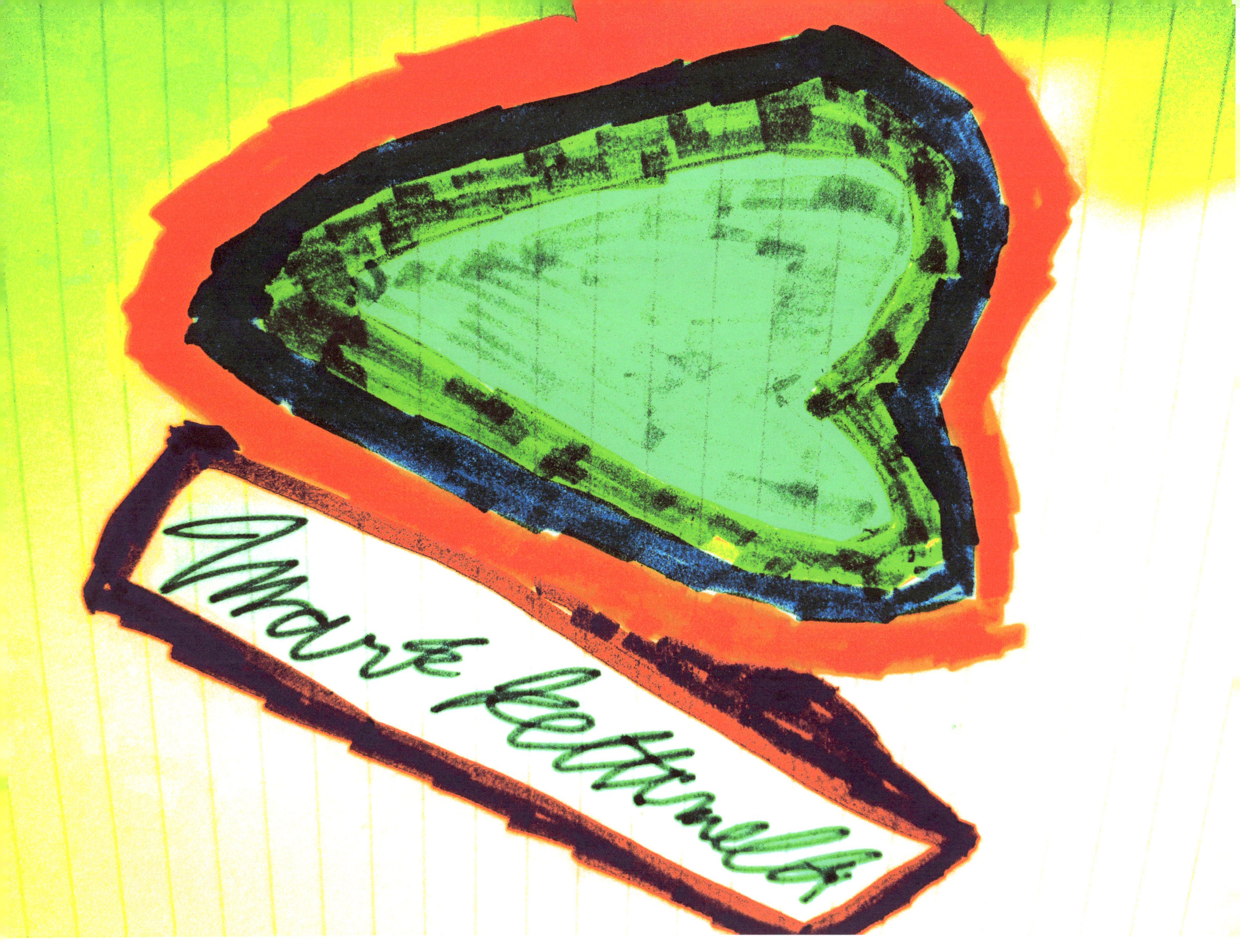

Marie Bettinelli

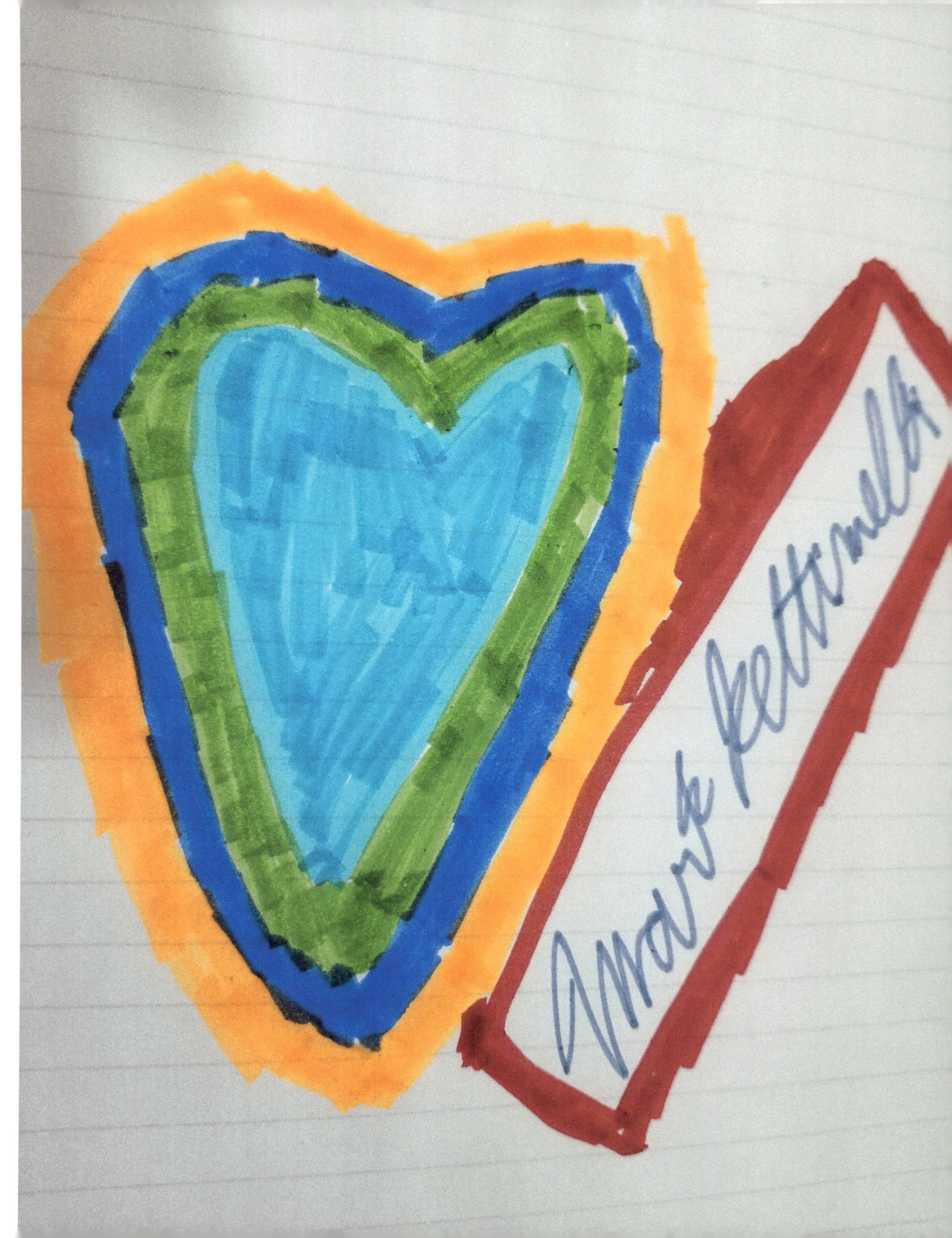

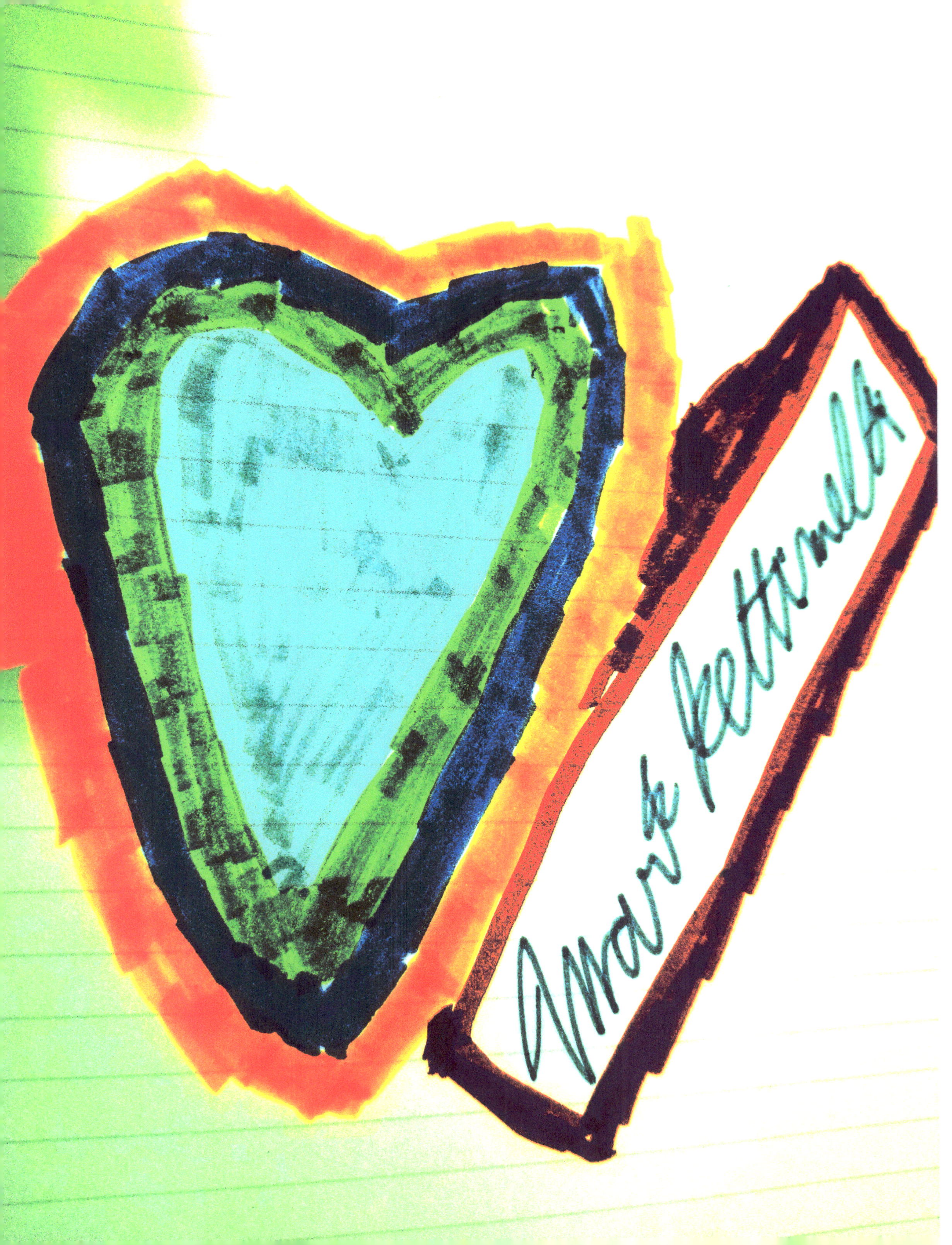

Mark Rettinelk
Mark Rettinelk
Mark Rettinelk

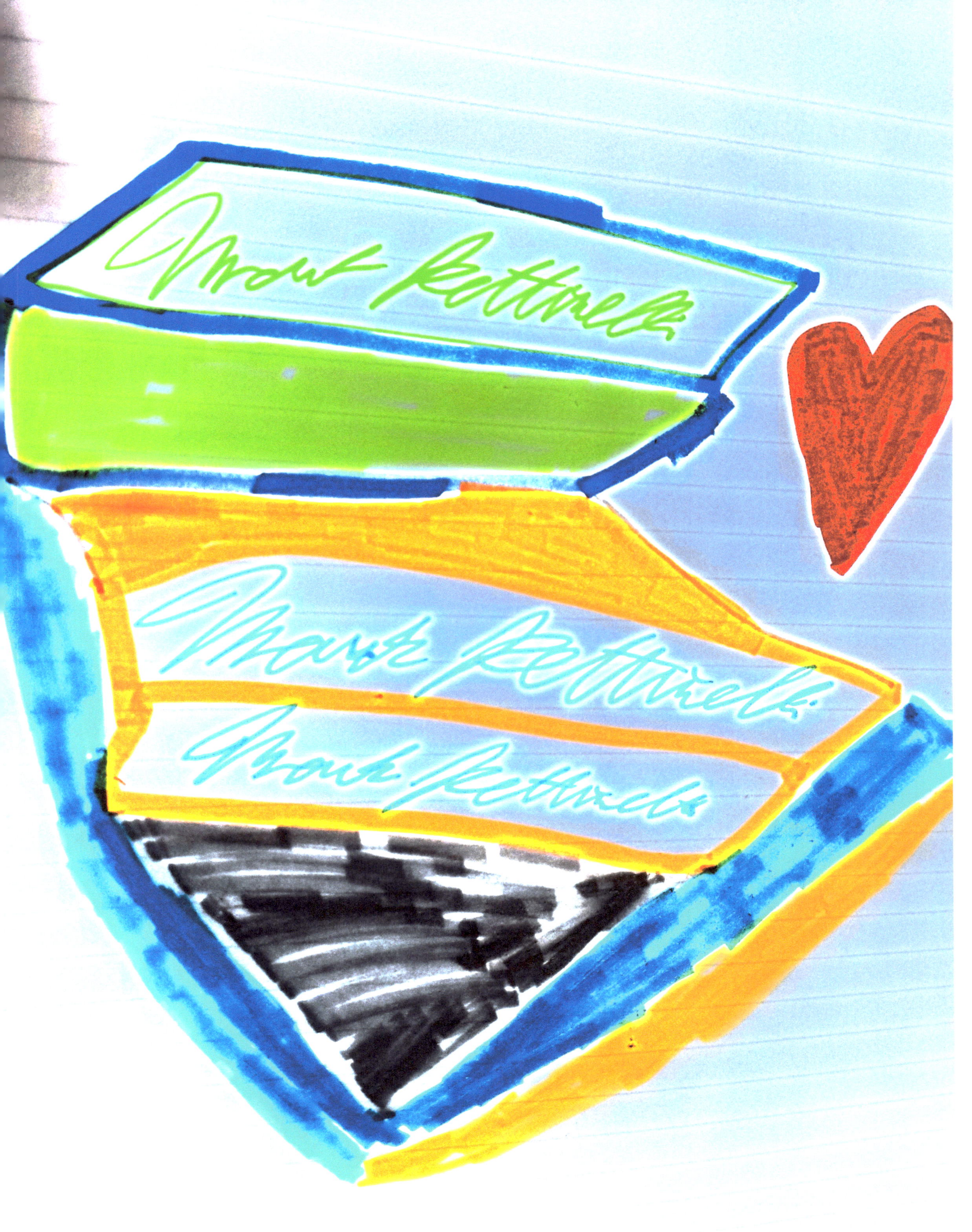

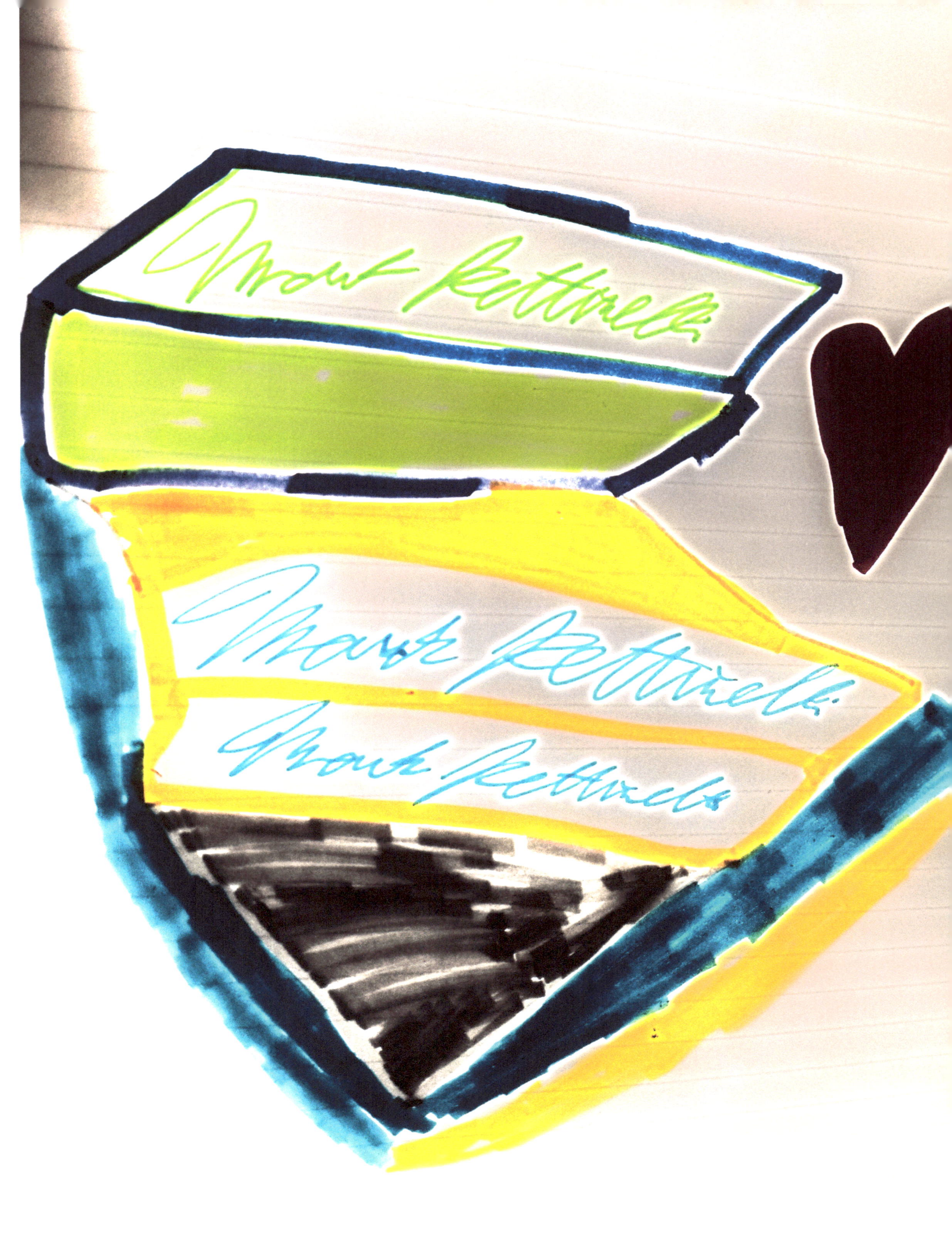

Mark Rettweli

Mark Rettweli

Mark Rettweli

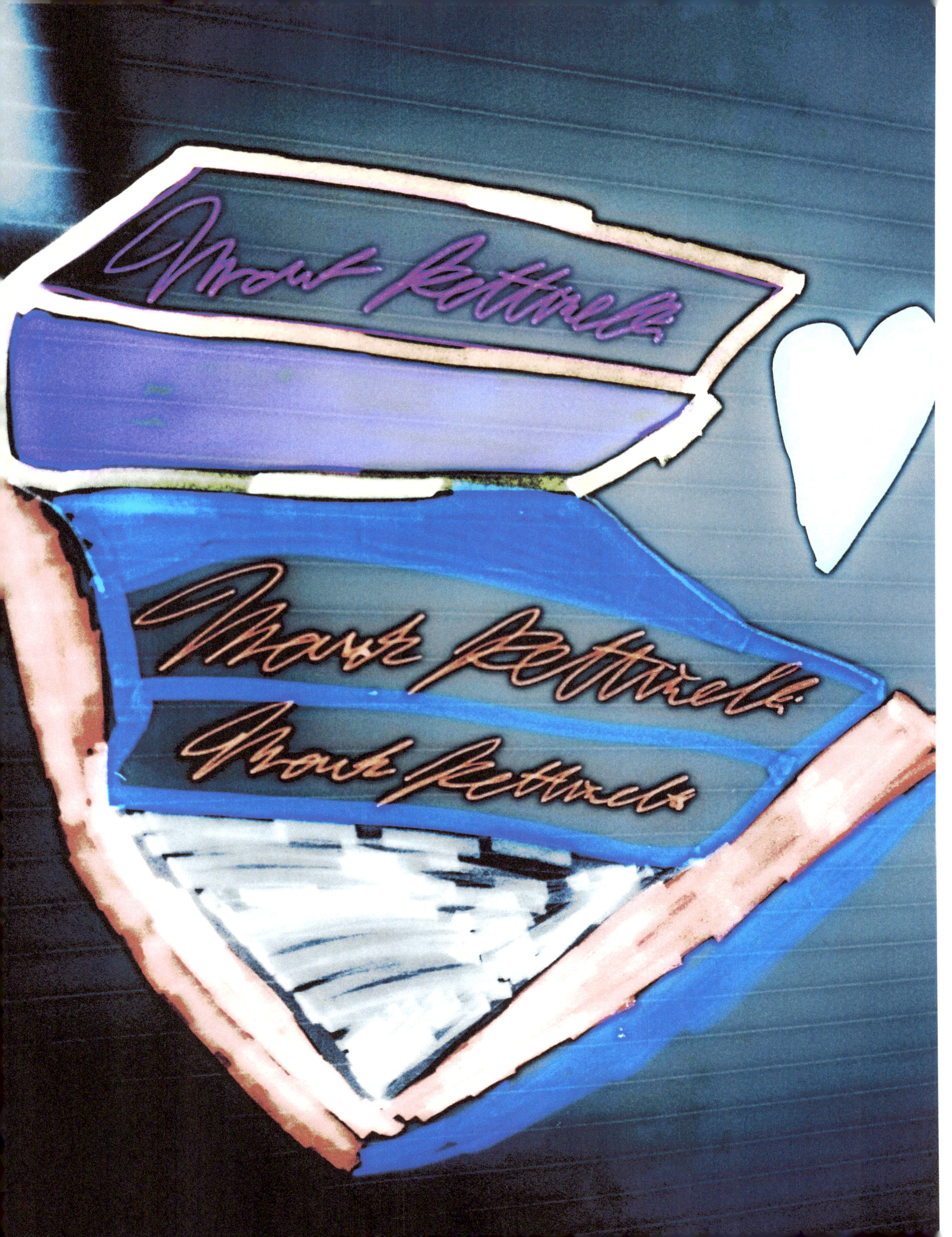

Mark Kostabi
Mark Kostabi
Mark Kostabi

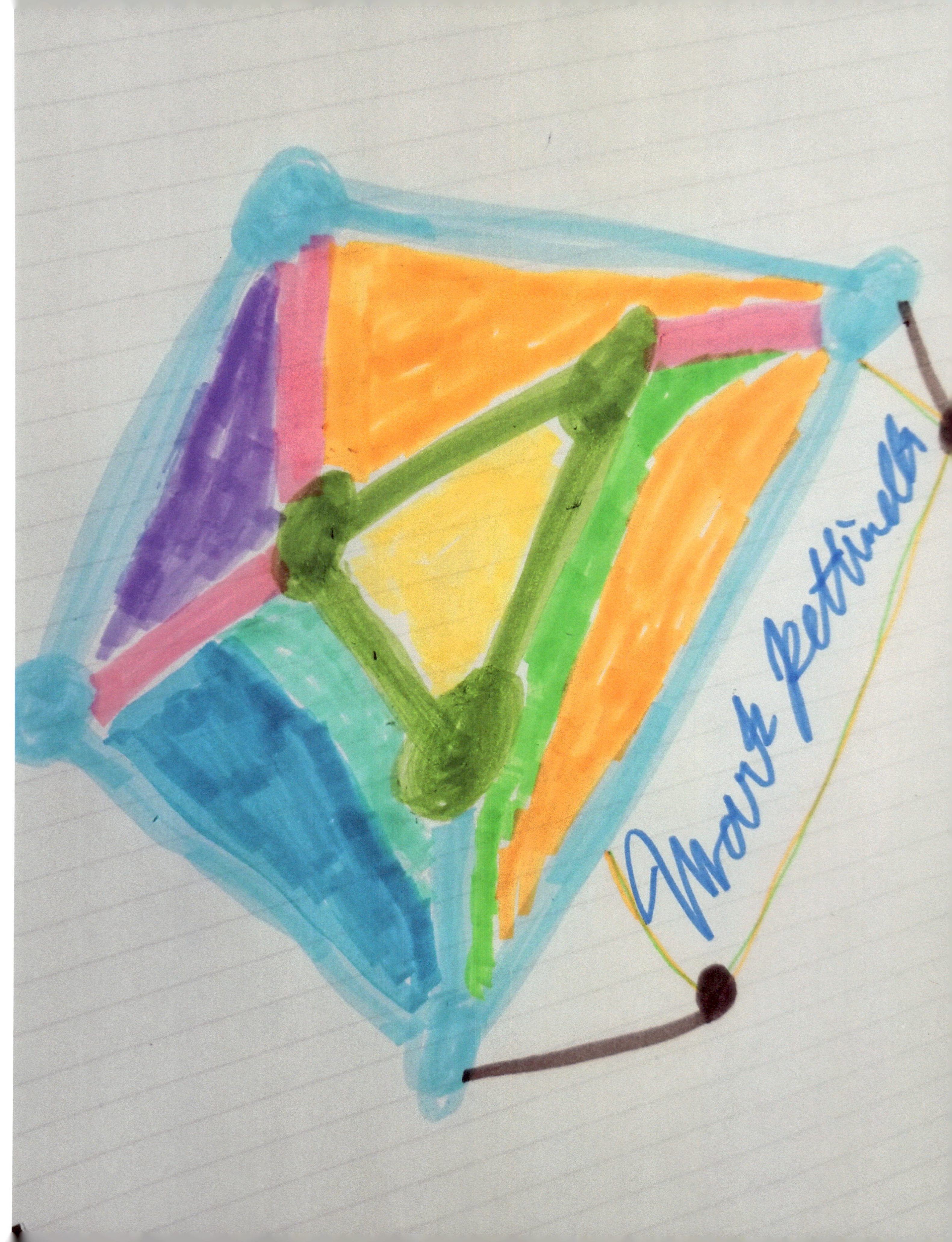
Mark Pettinella

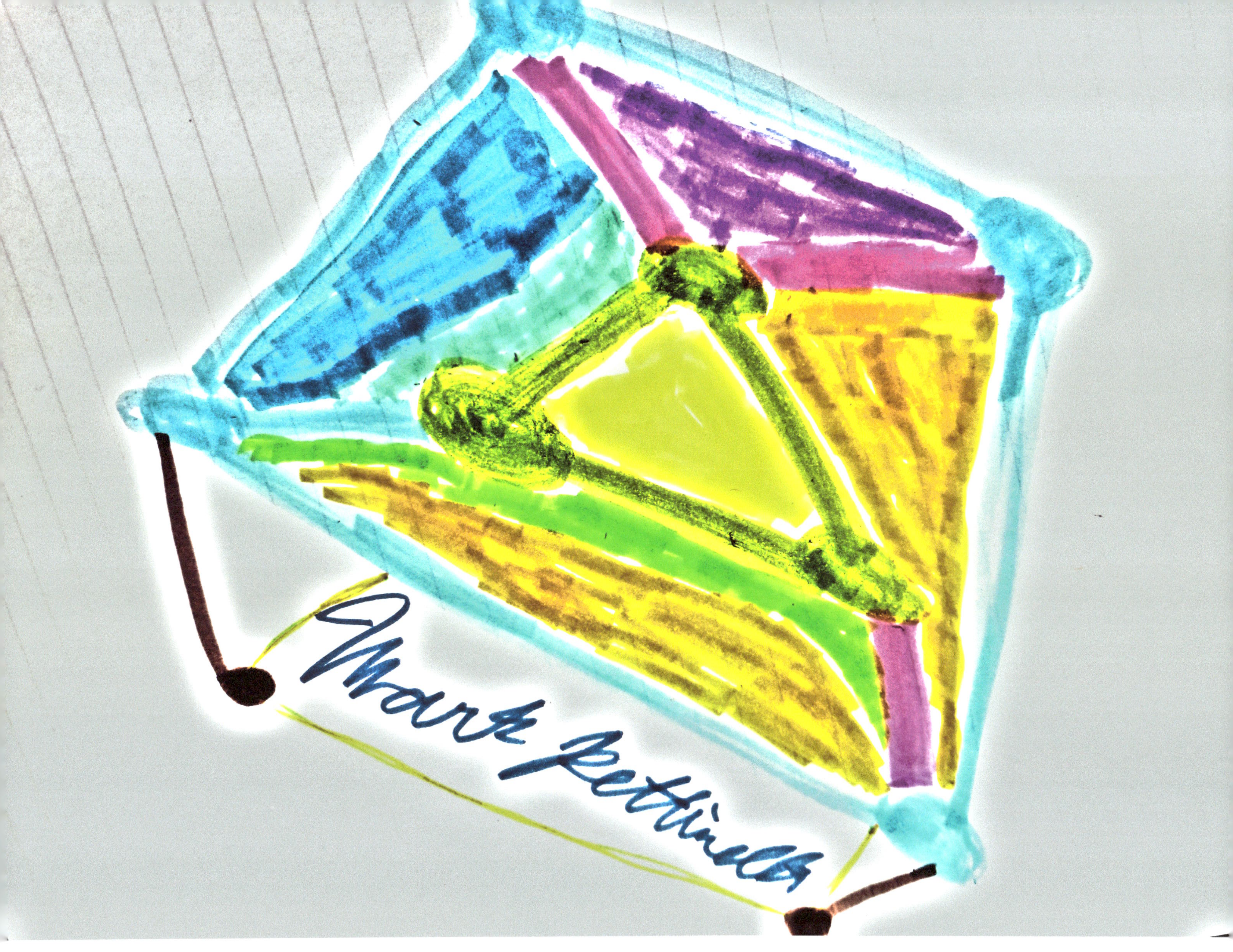
Mark Pettinelli

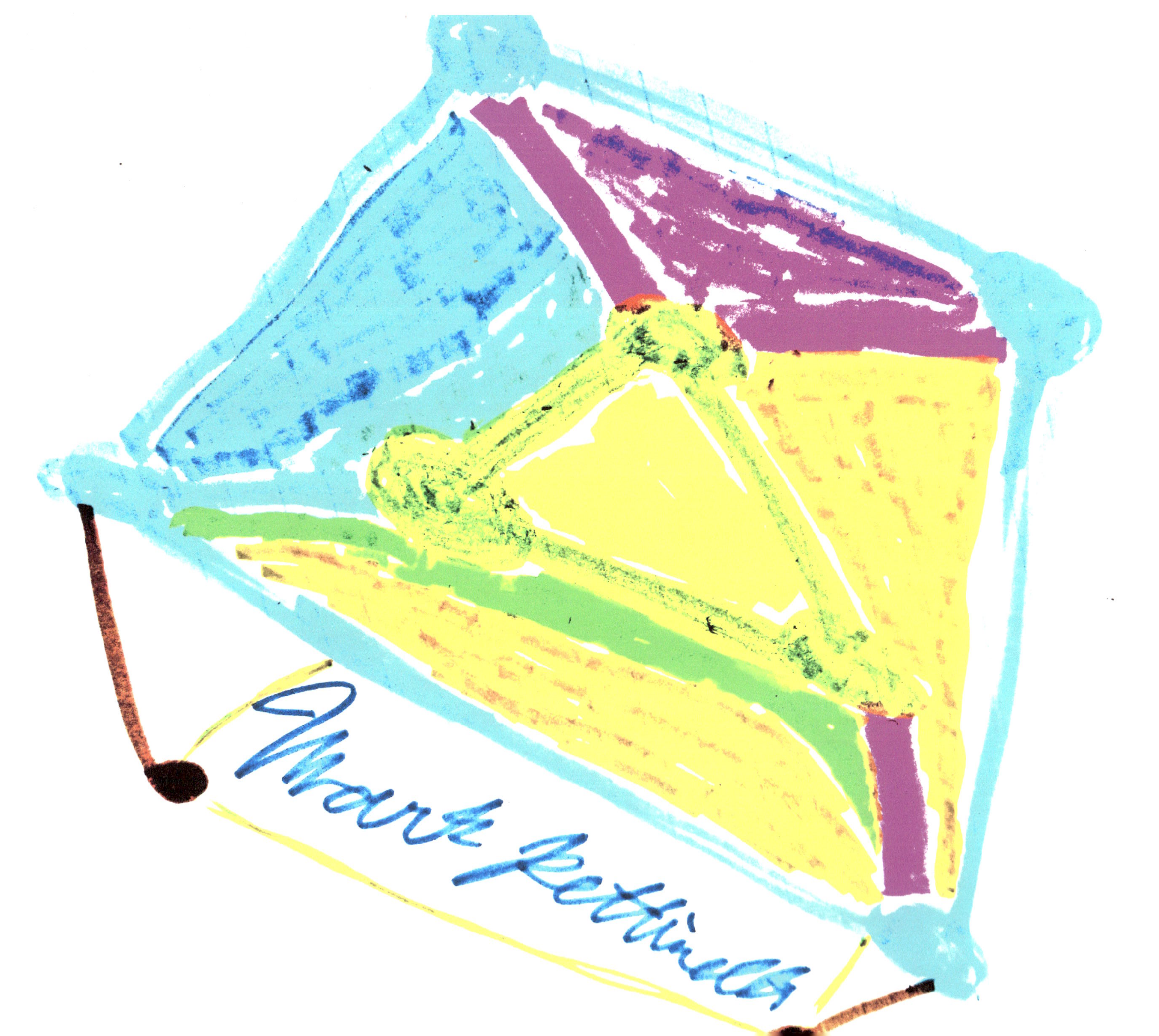
Mark Pettinella

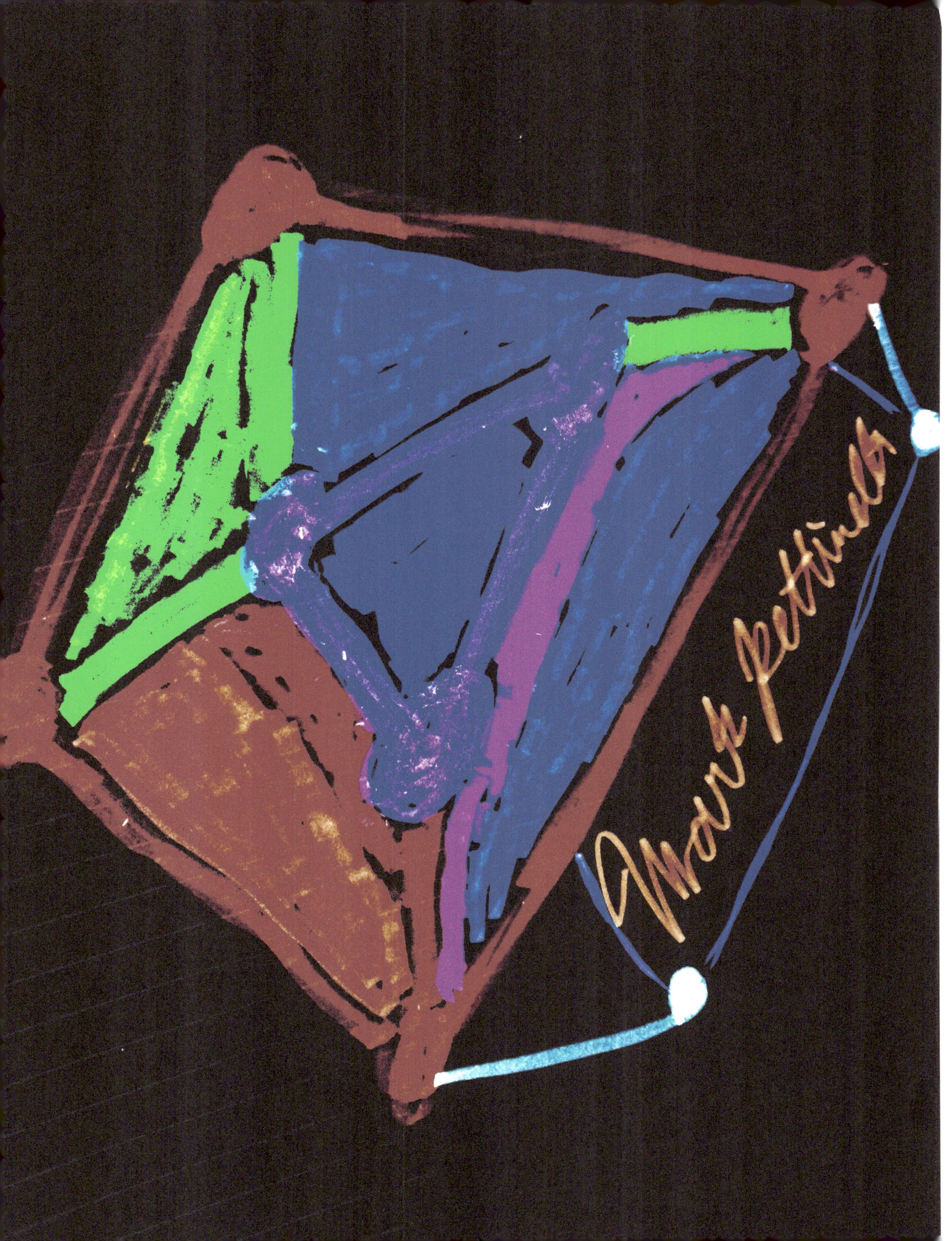

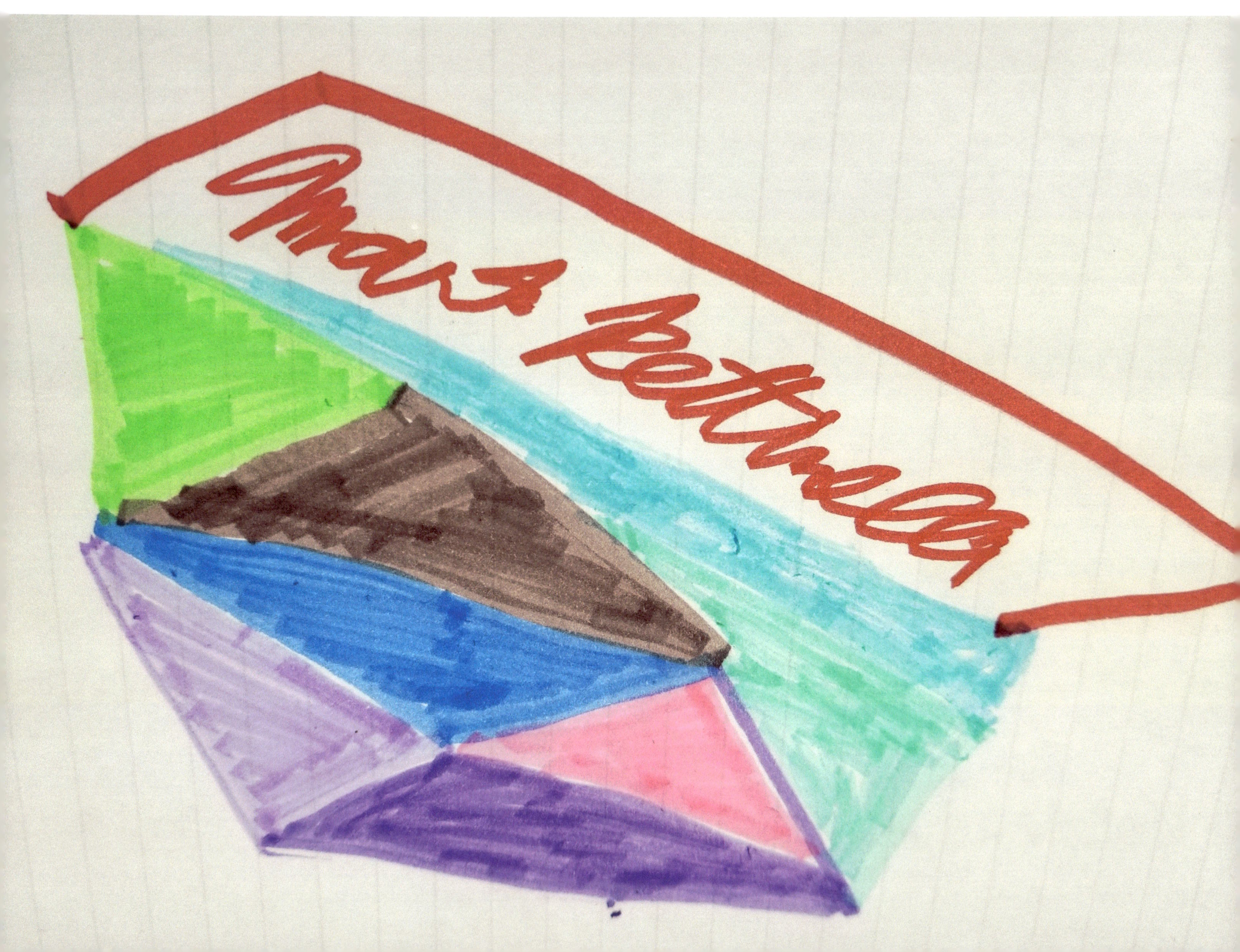
Omar Pettinelli

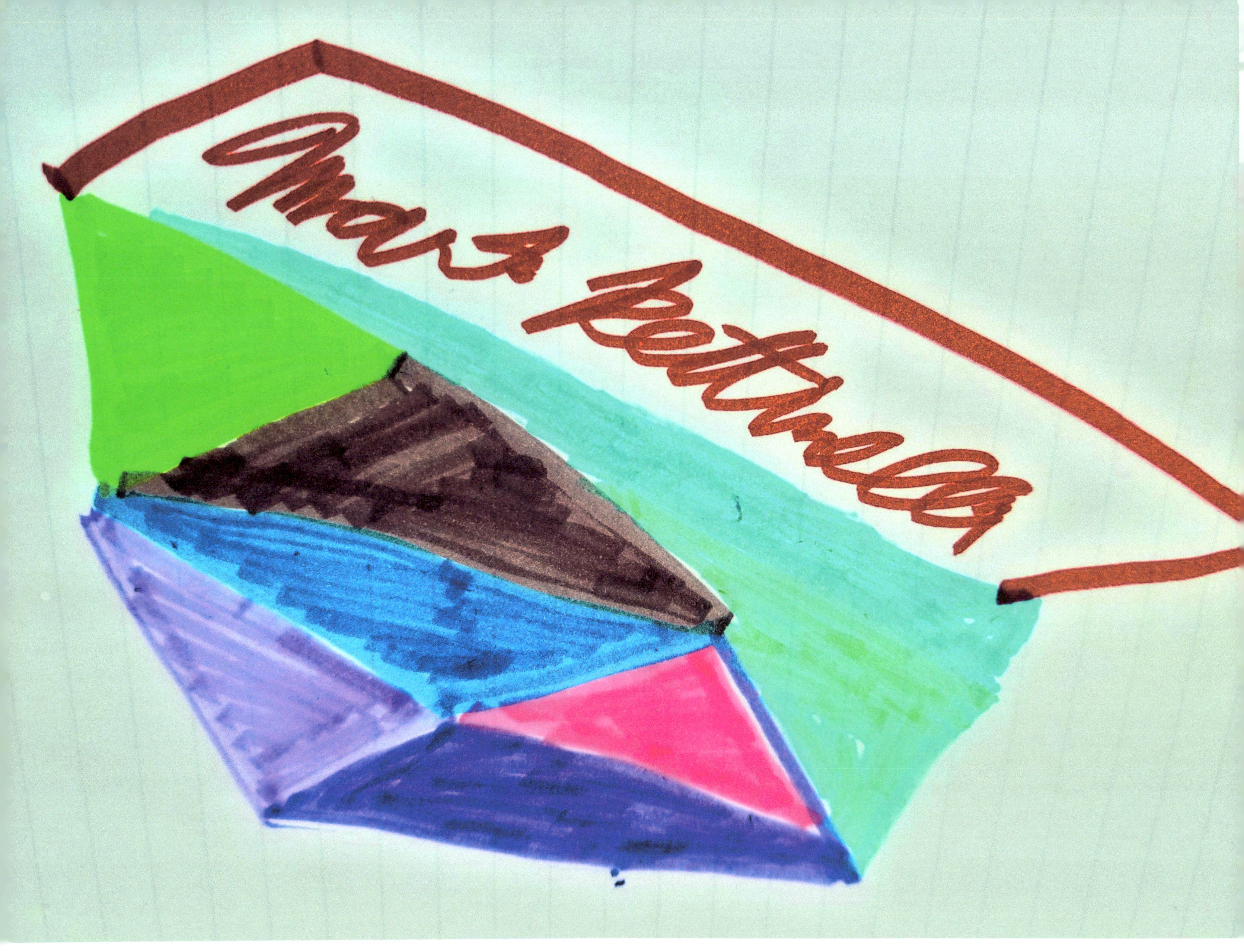
Mars Pettrula

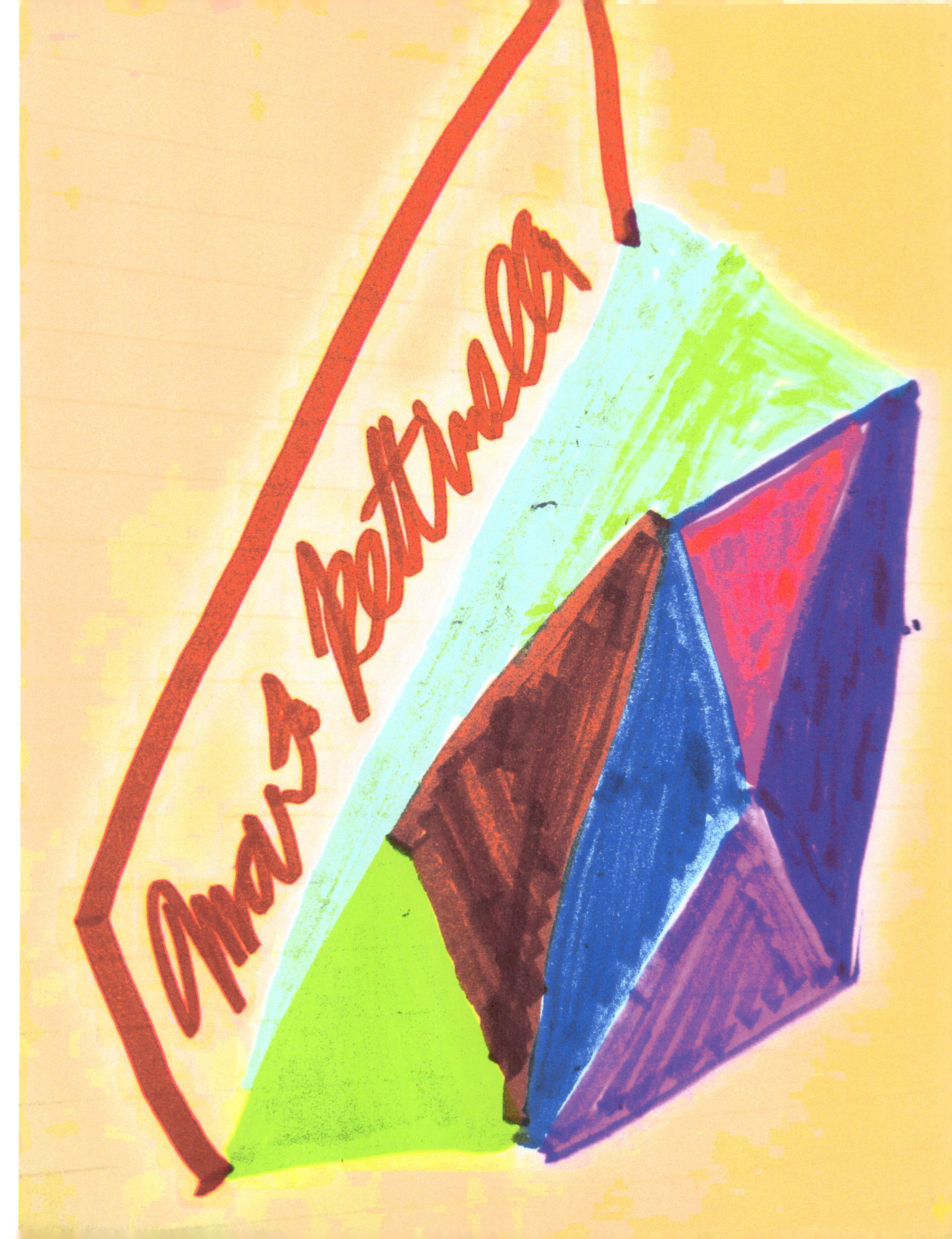

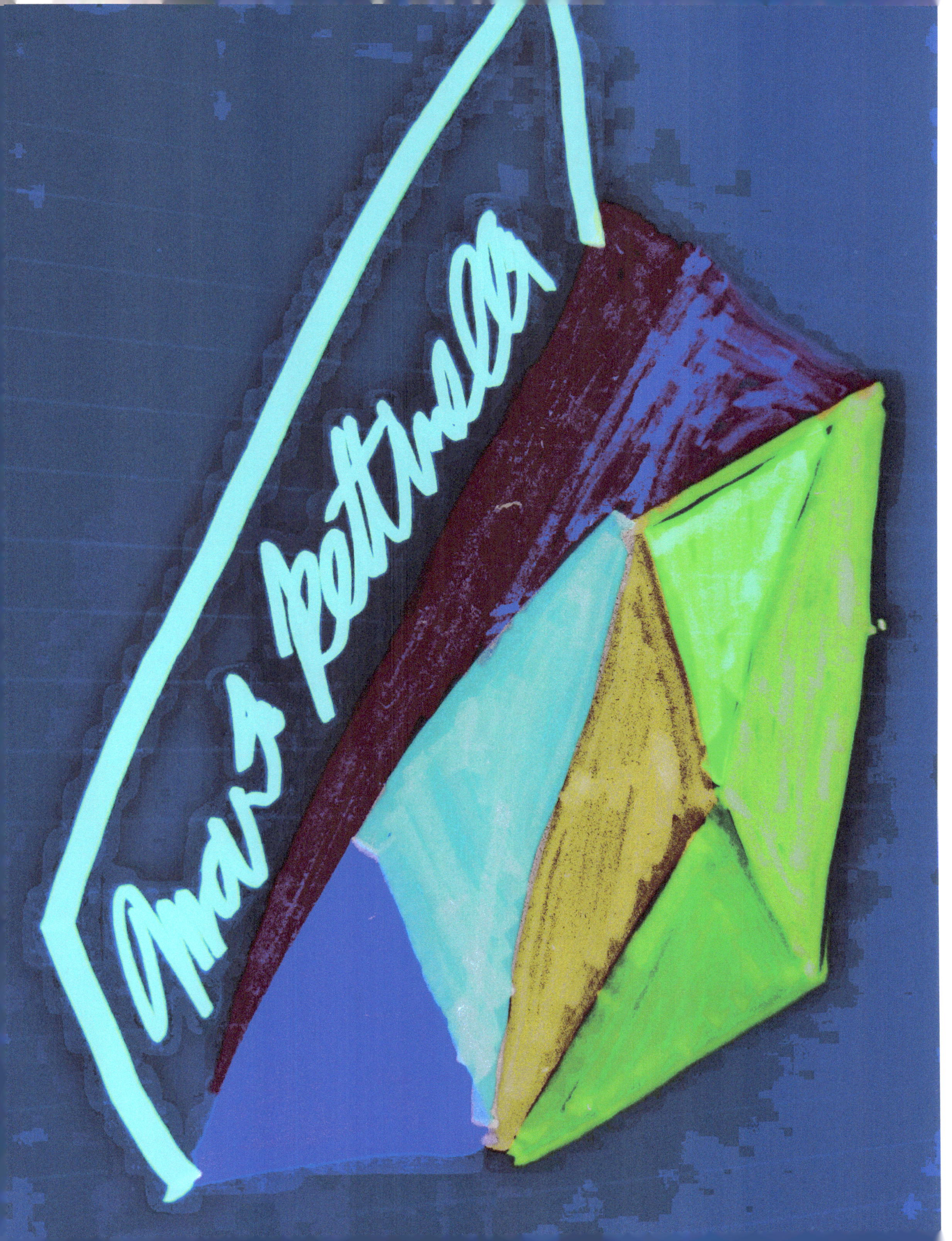

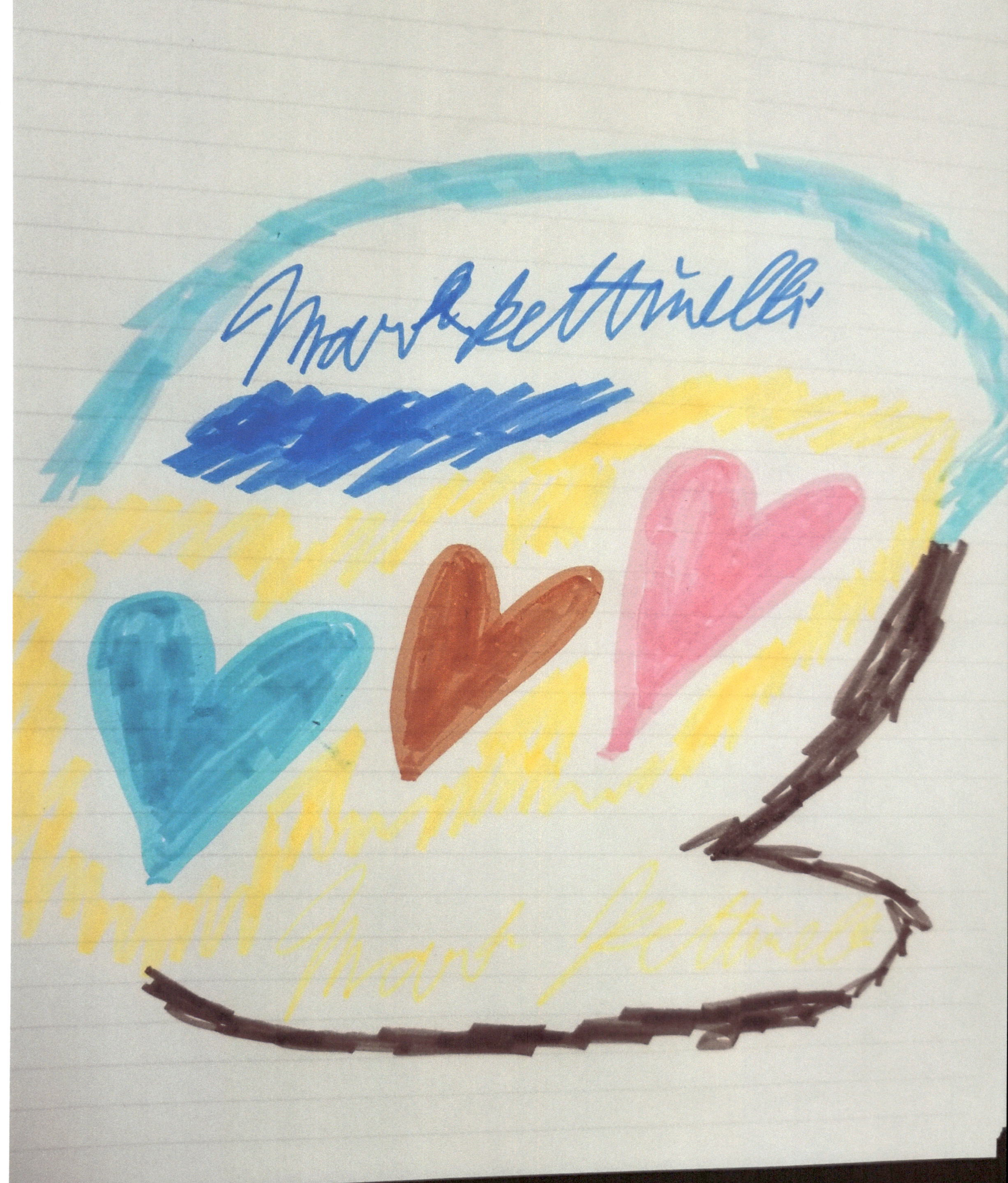
Mark Kettiniller

Marckettiuelli

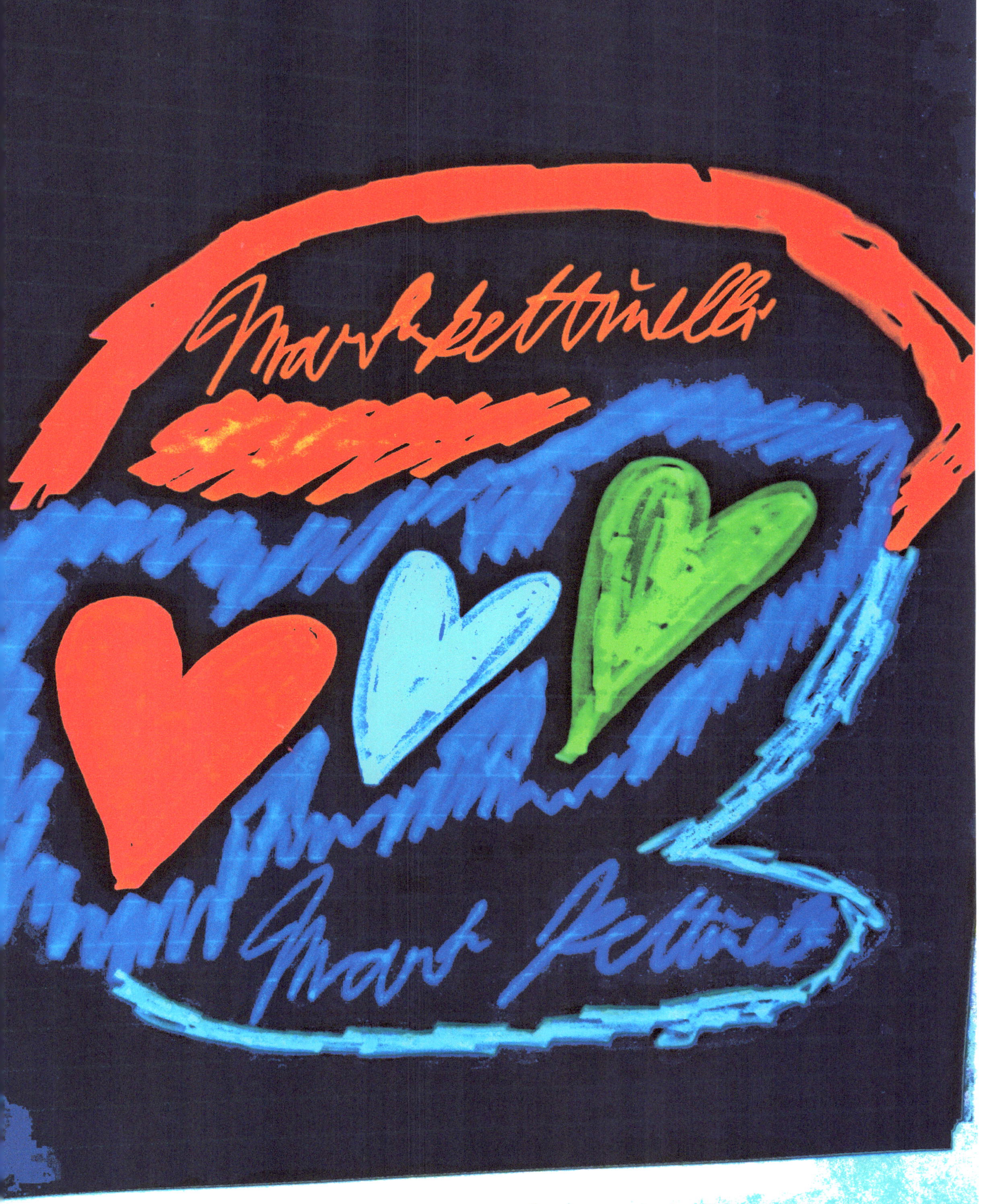
Markettinelli
Mark Kostabi

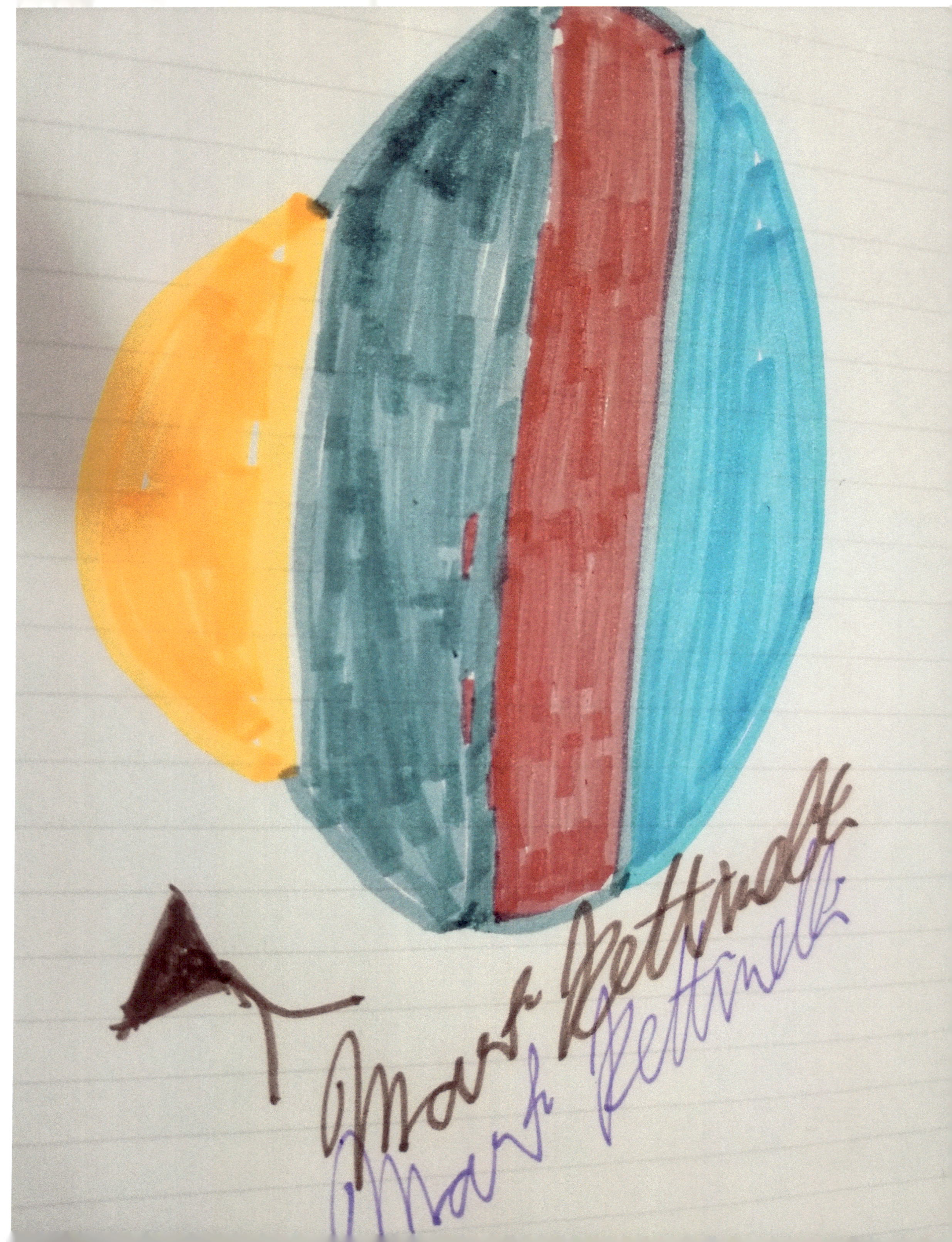

Mark Rettinoff
Mark Rettinelli

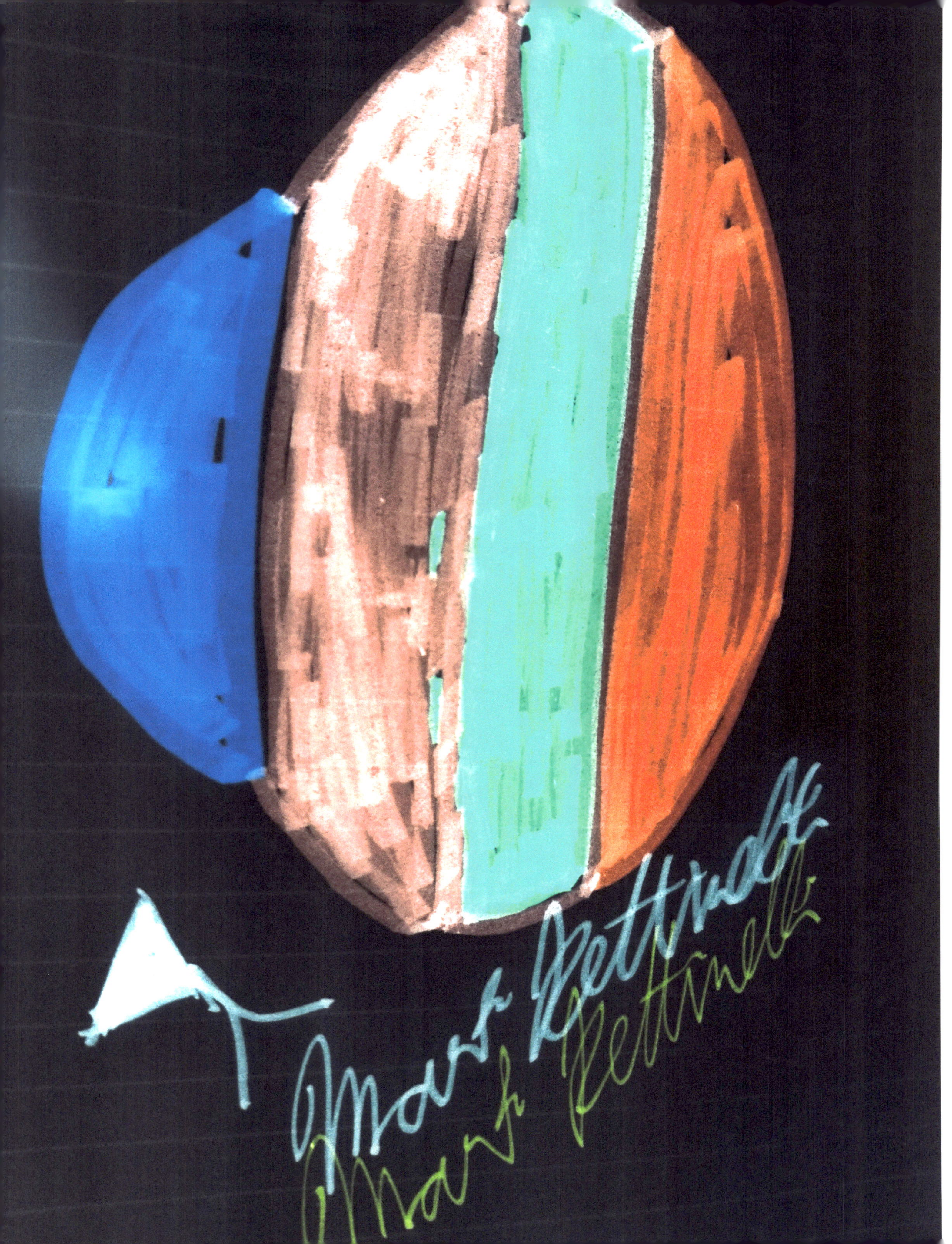
Mark Rettrodt
Mark Rettinelli

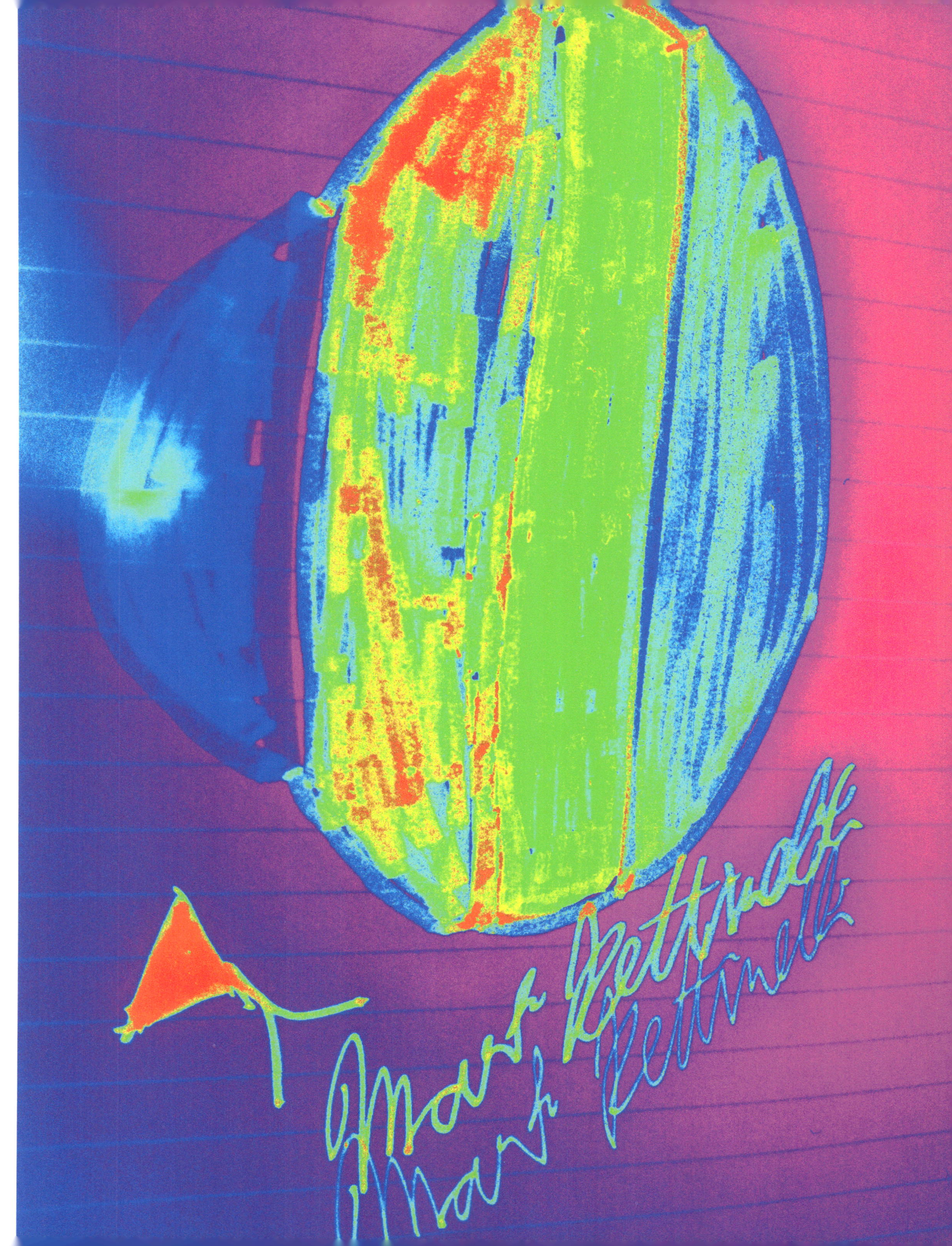

Mark Rettindt
Mark Rettindt

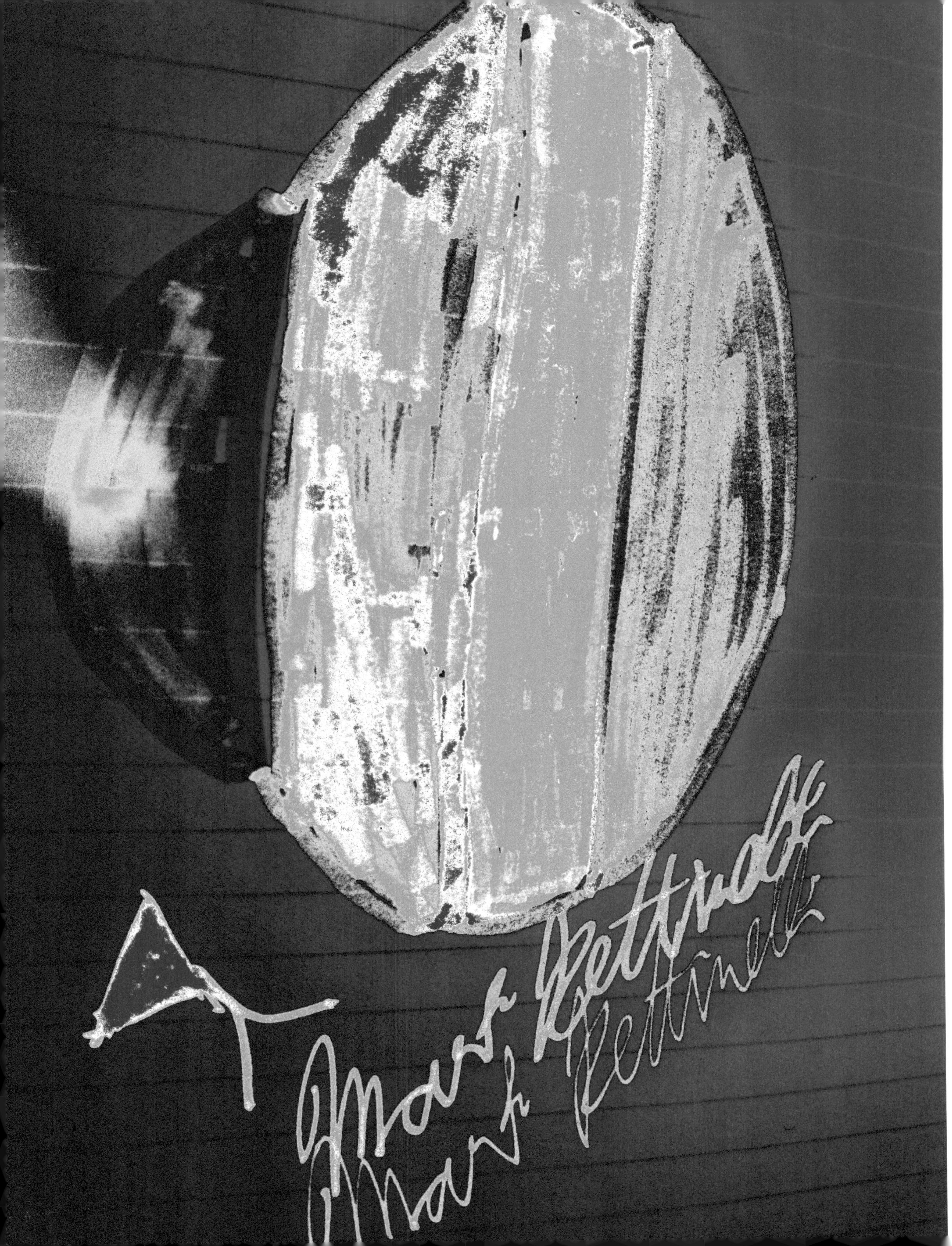
Mark Bettridge
Mark Bettridge

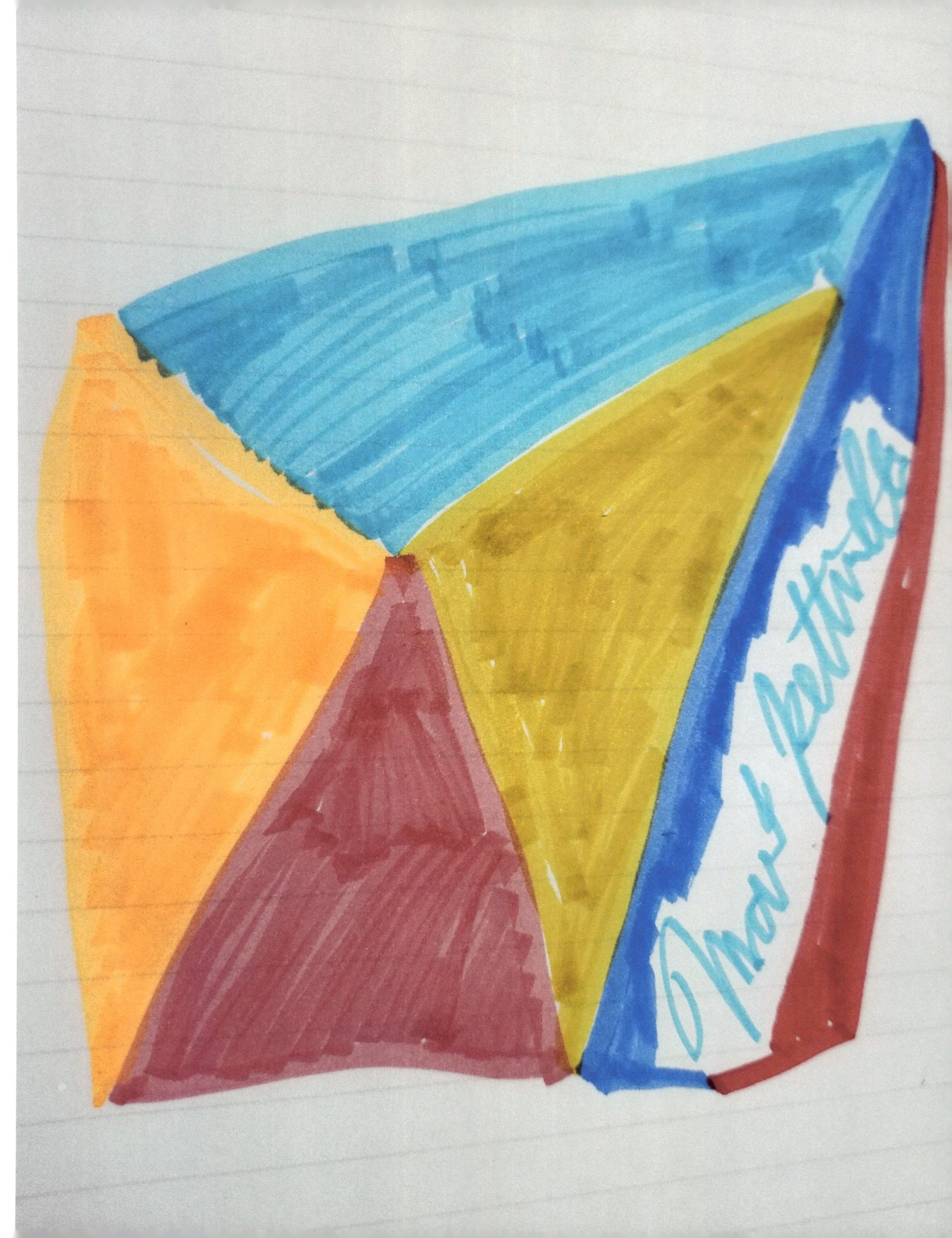

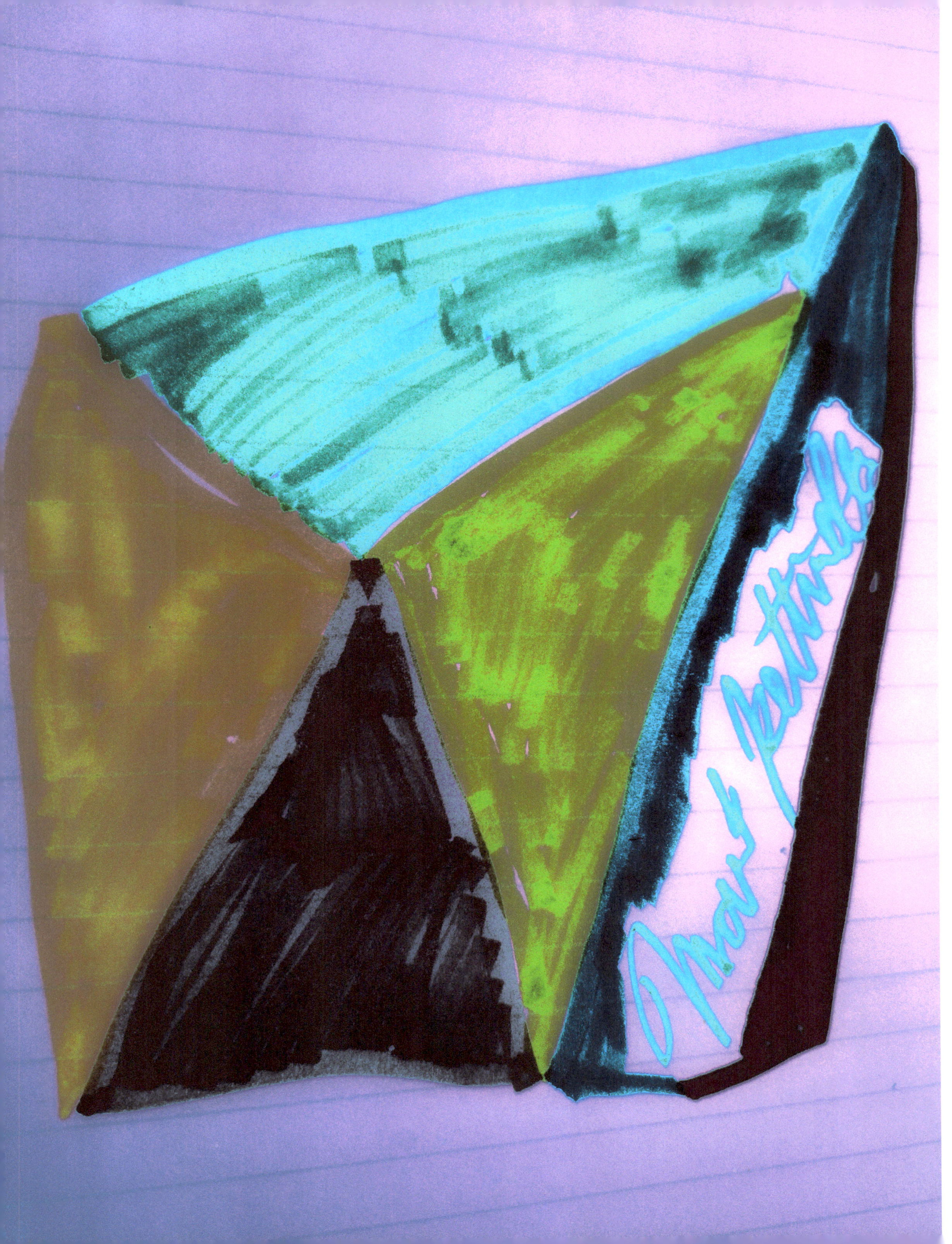
Omar Bertinelli

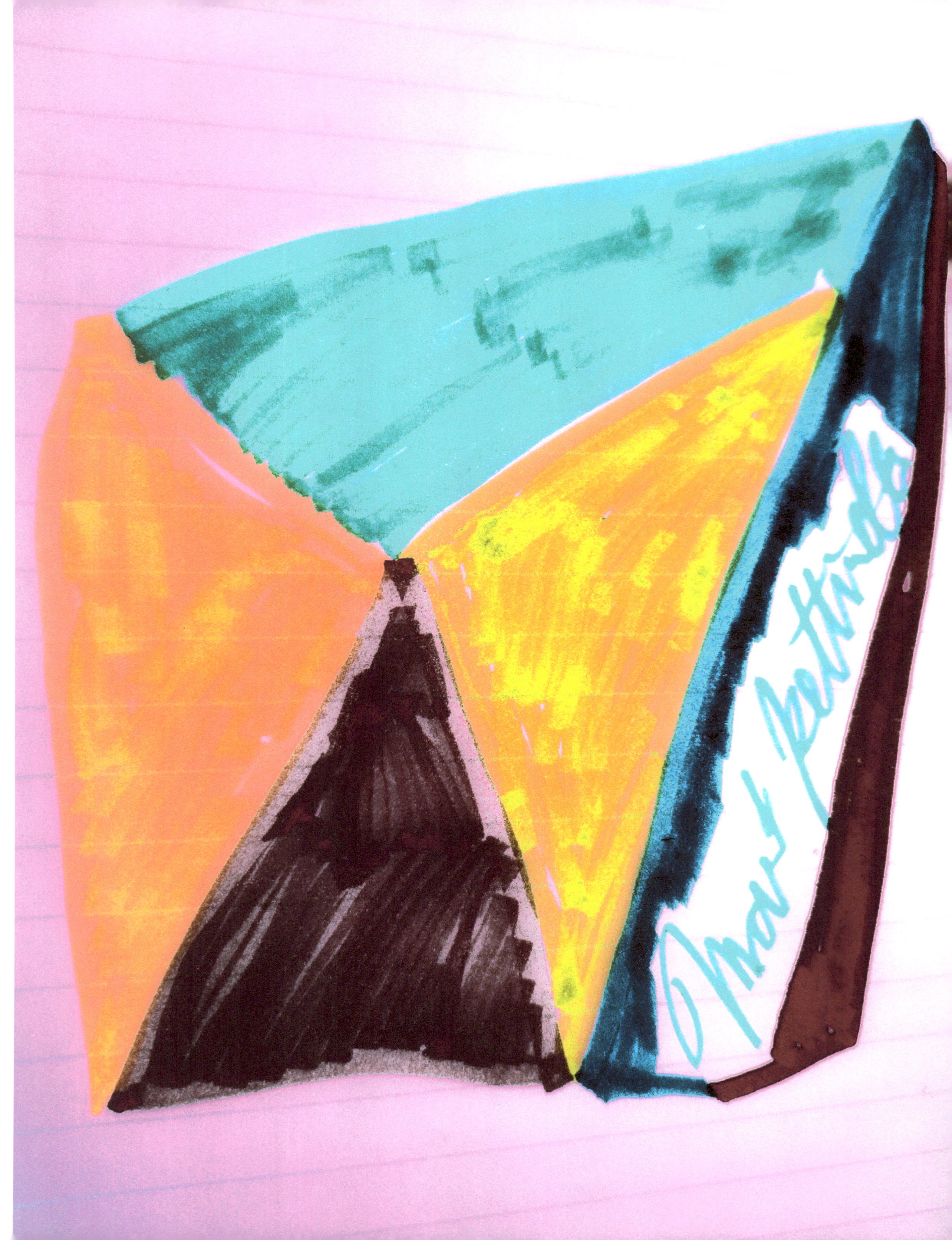
Mark Bertula

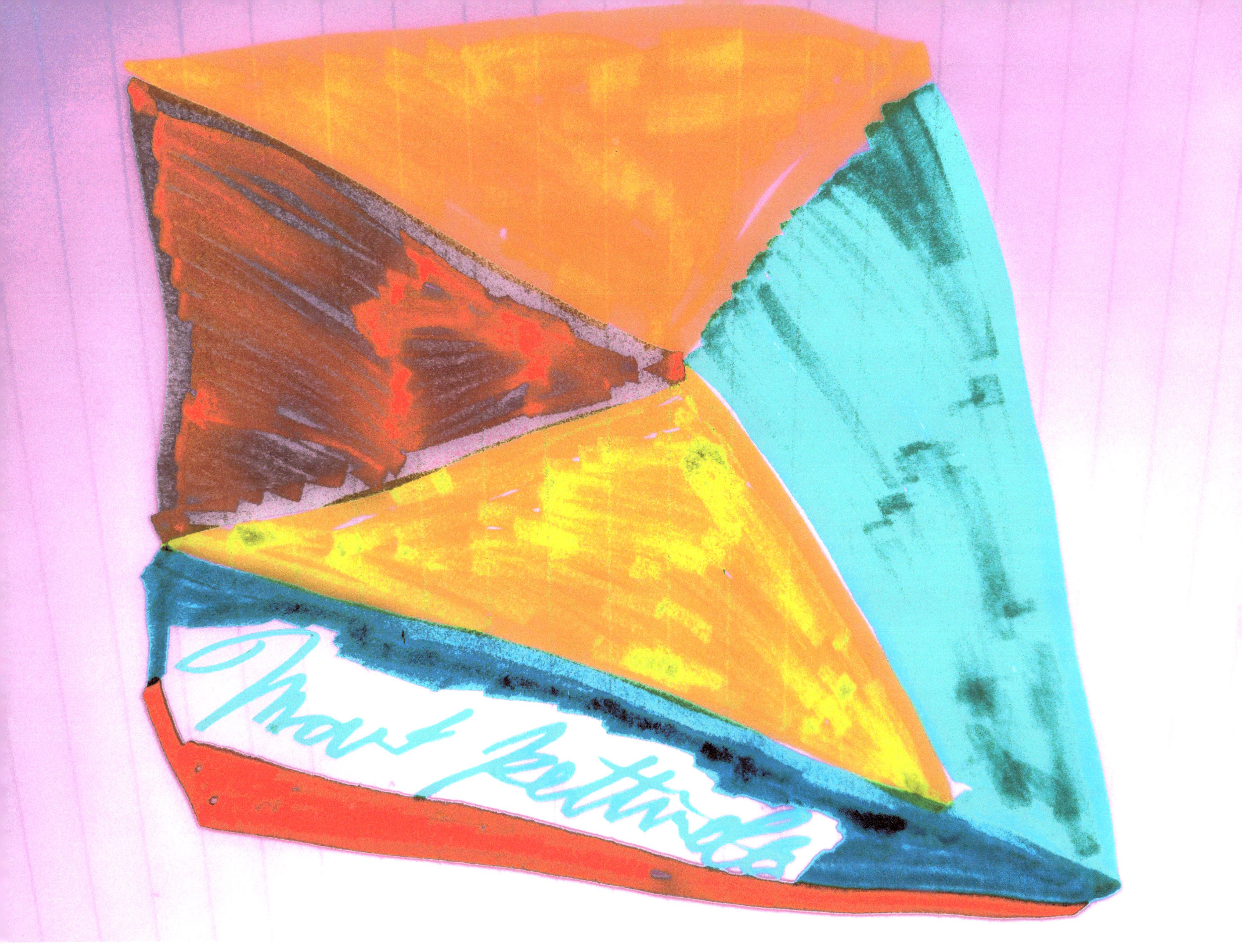
Mart Bethards

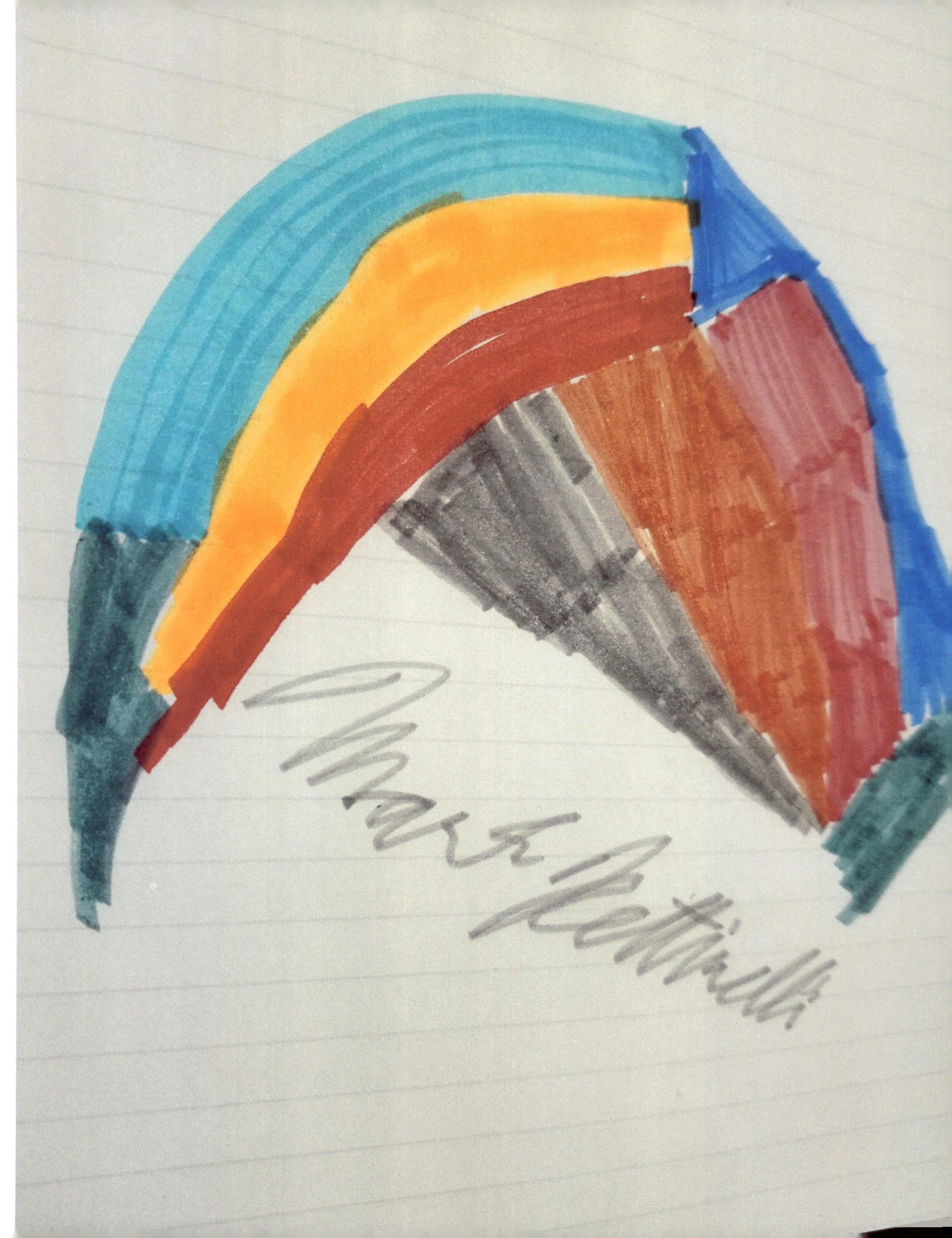

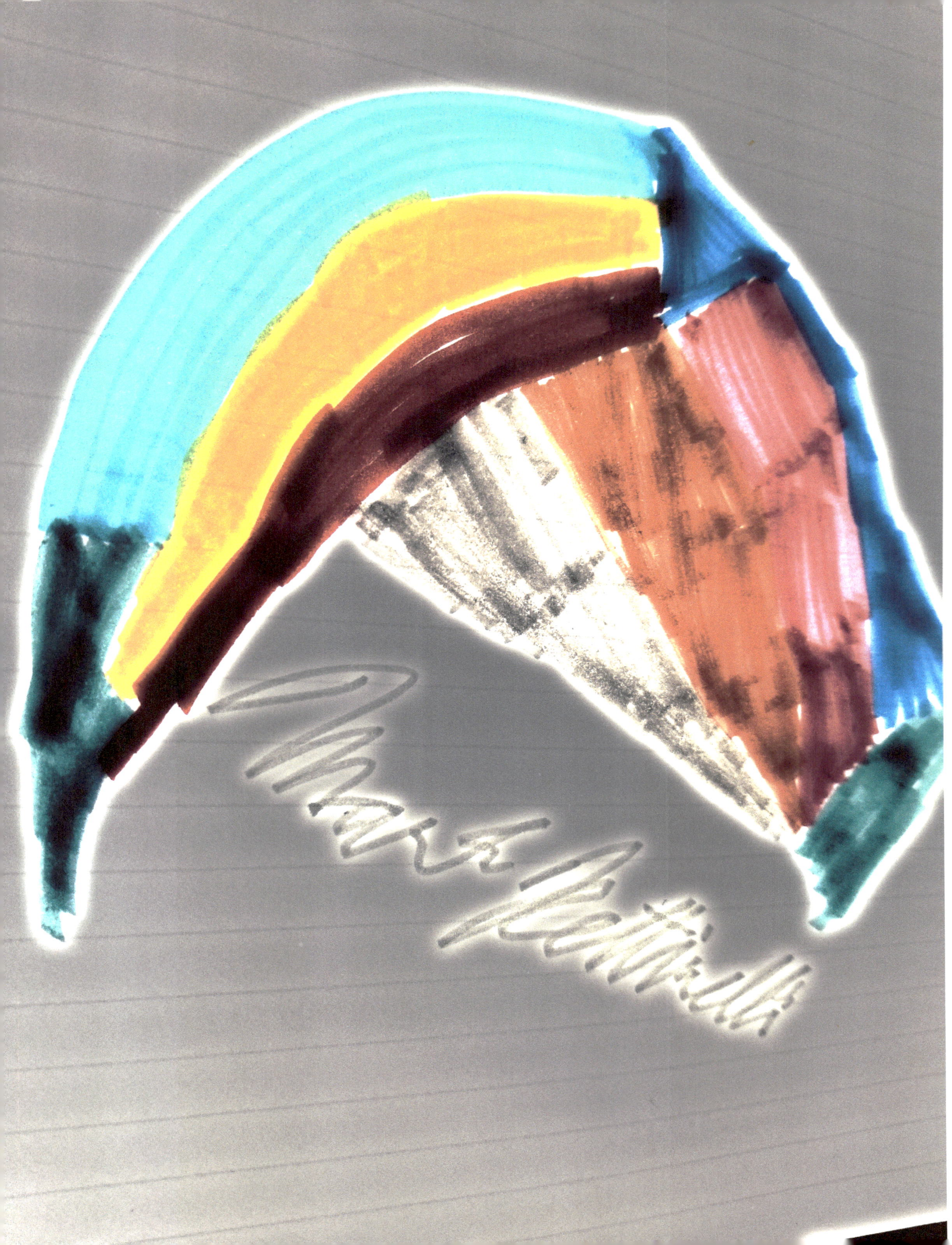

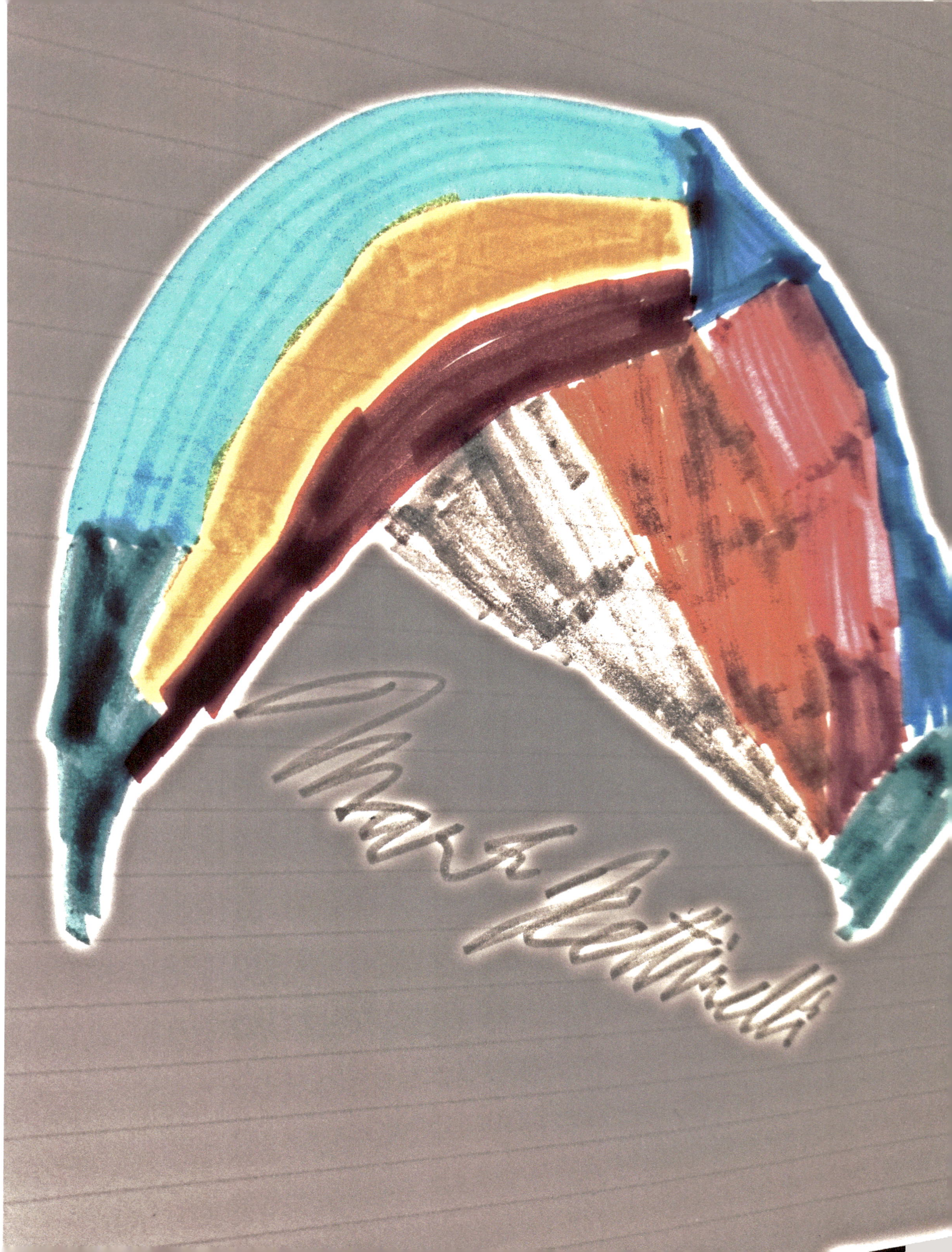

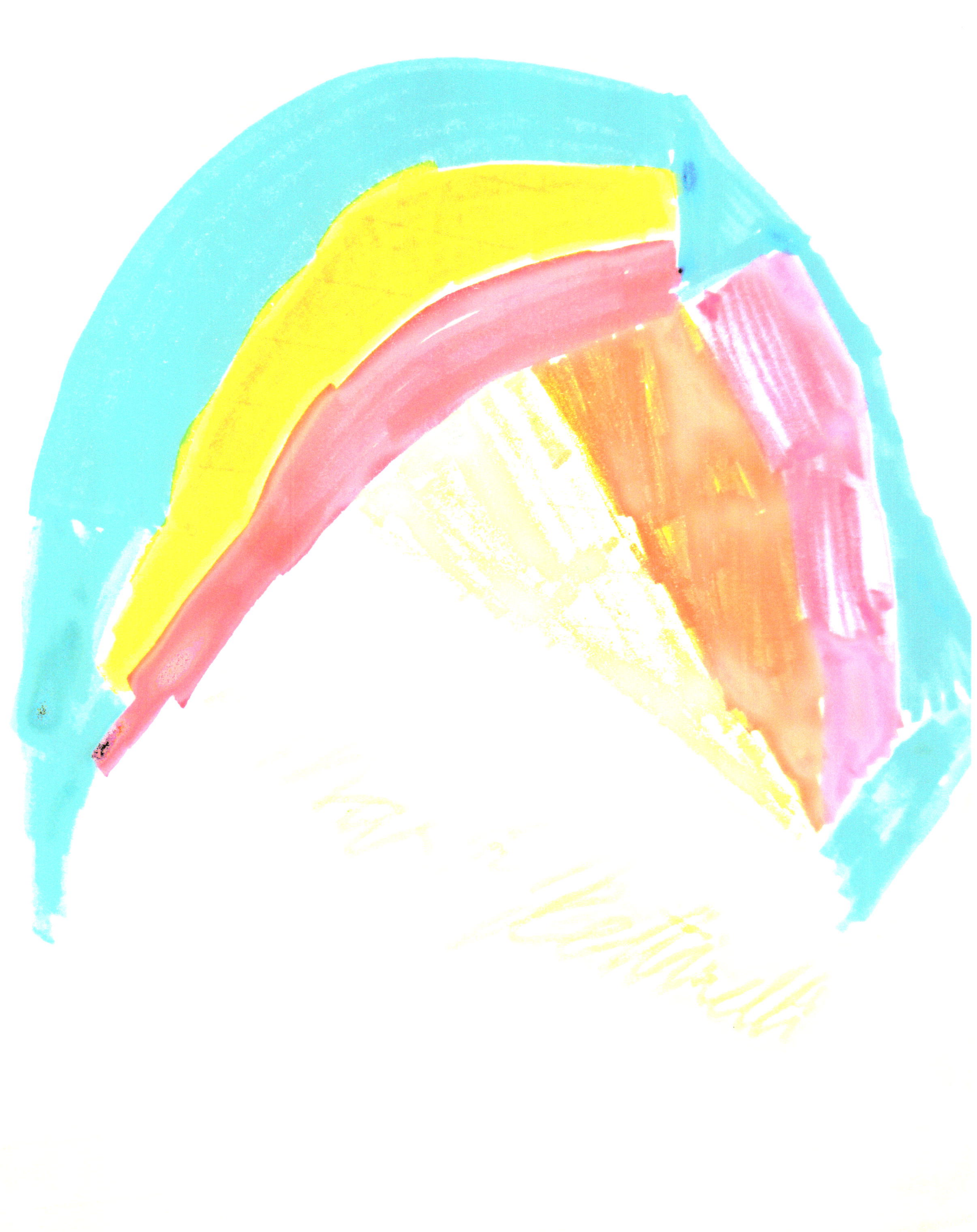

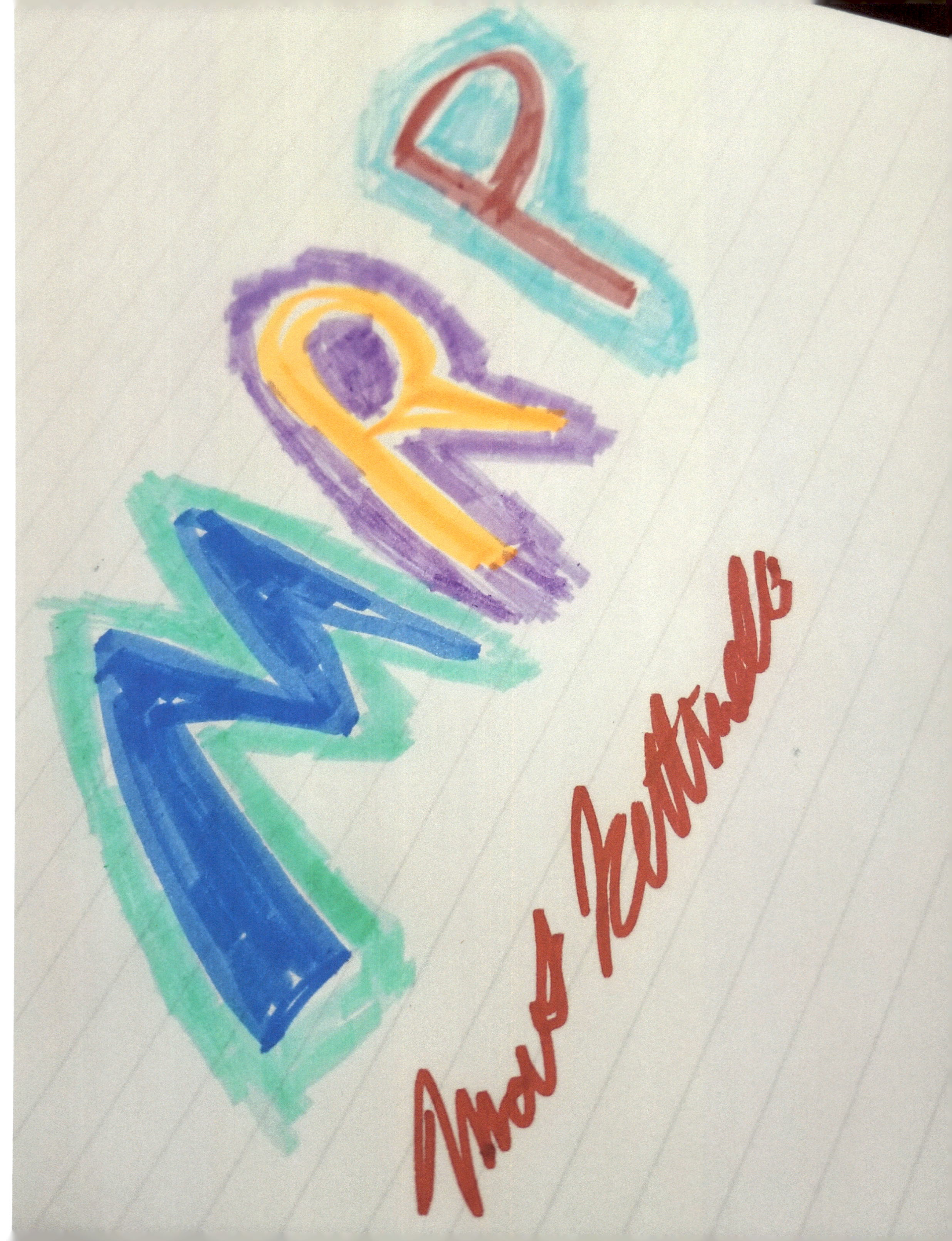

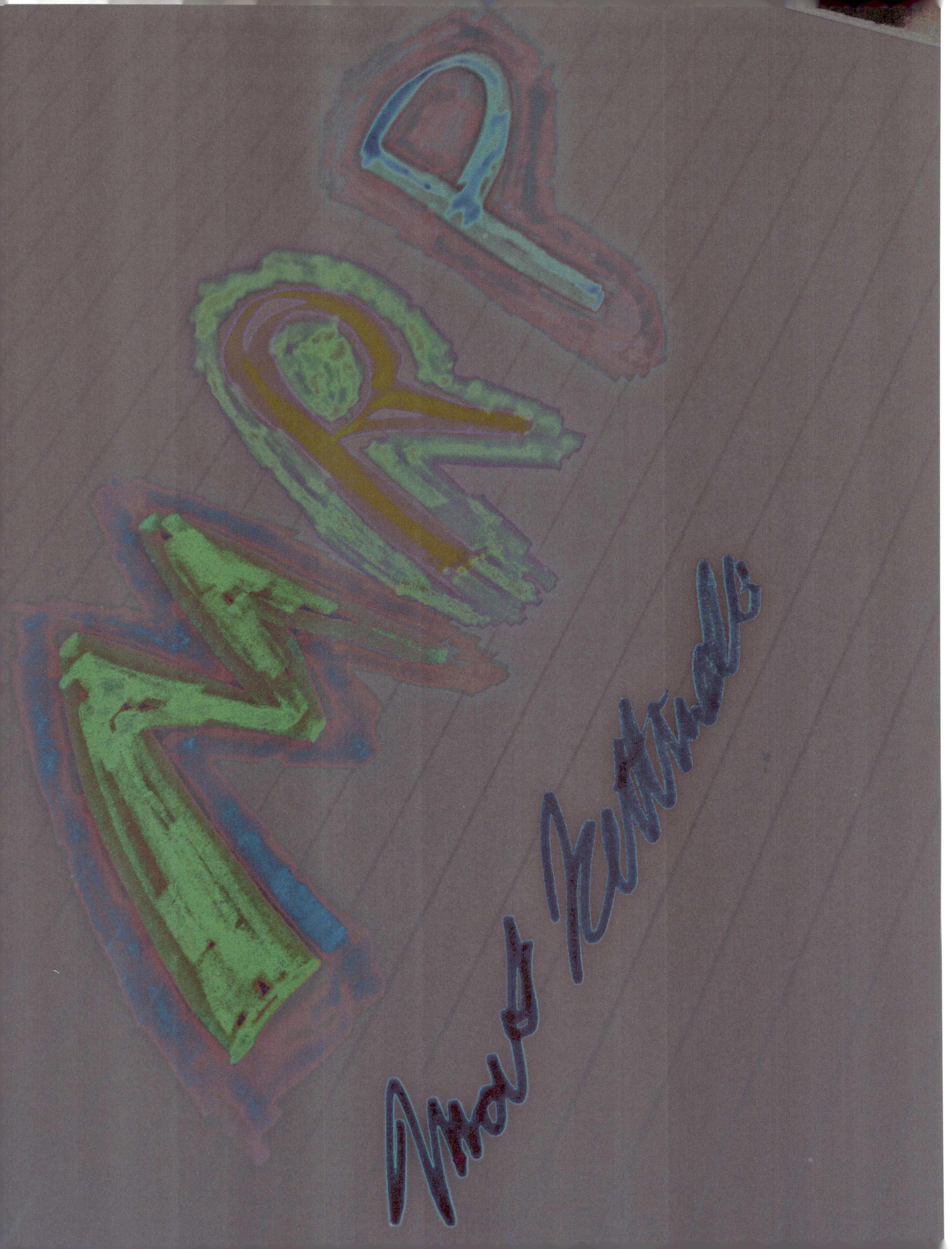

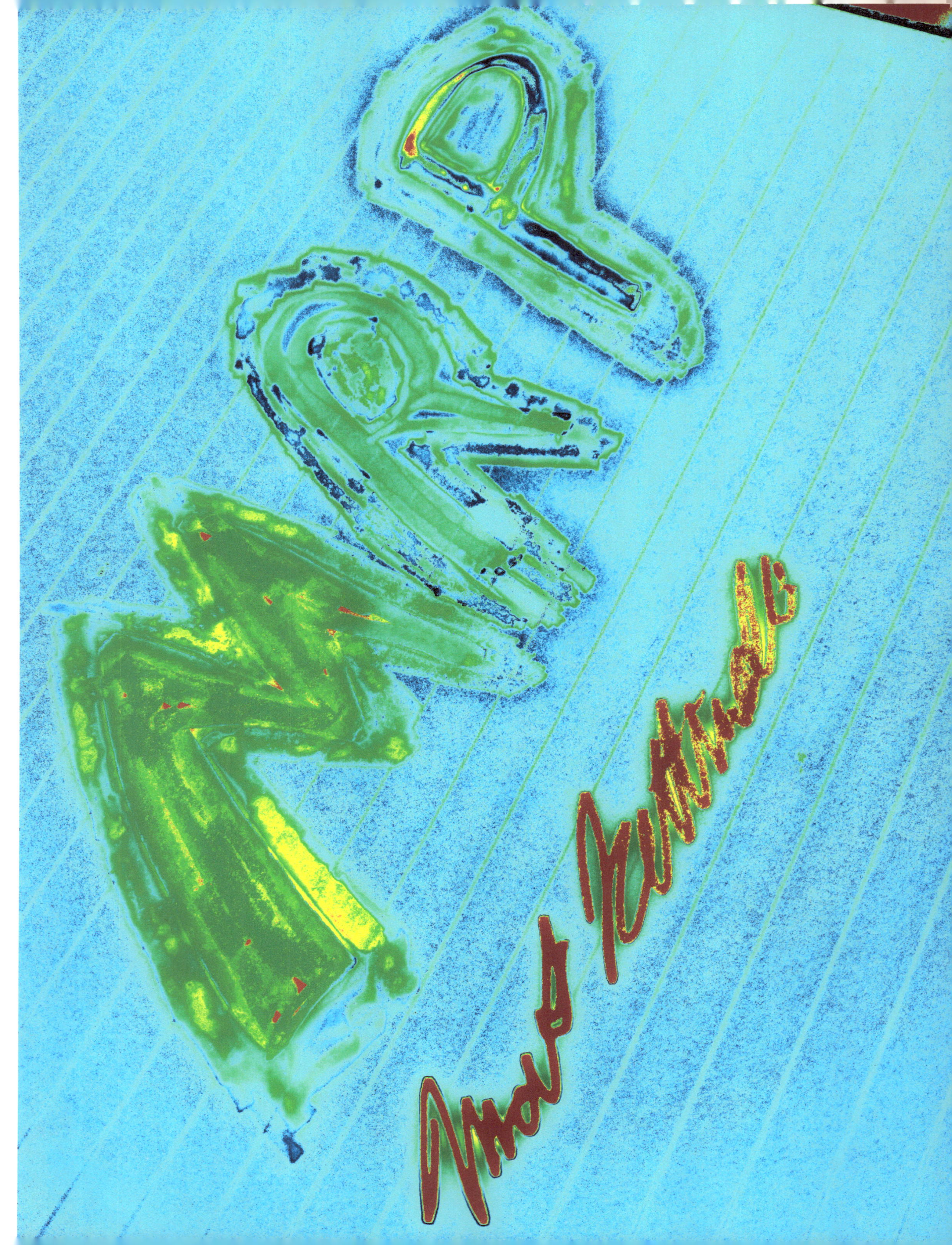

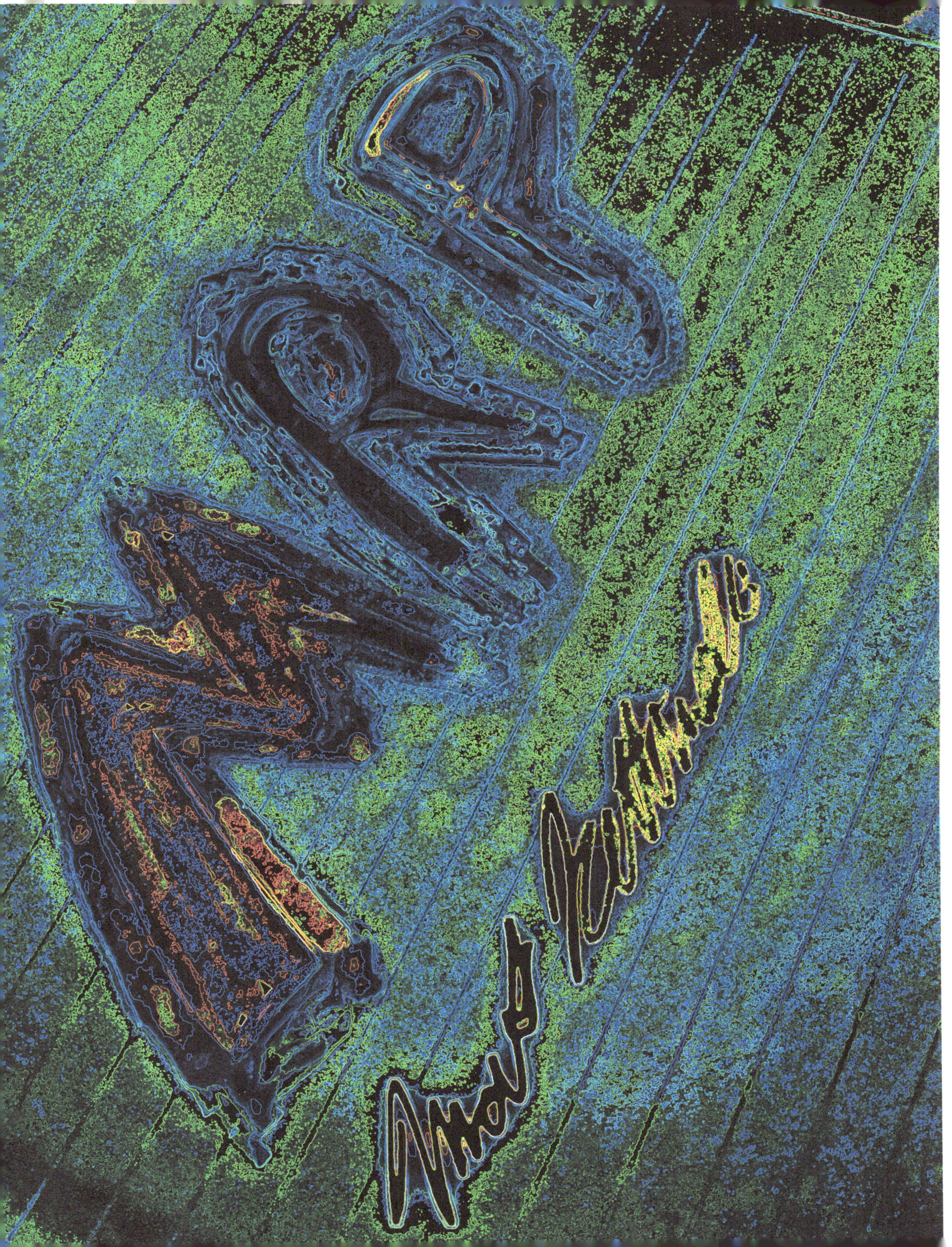

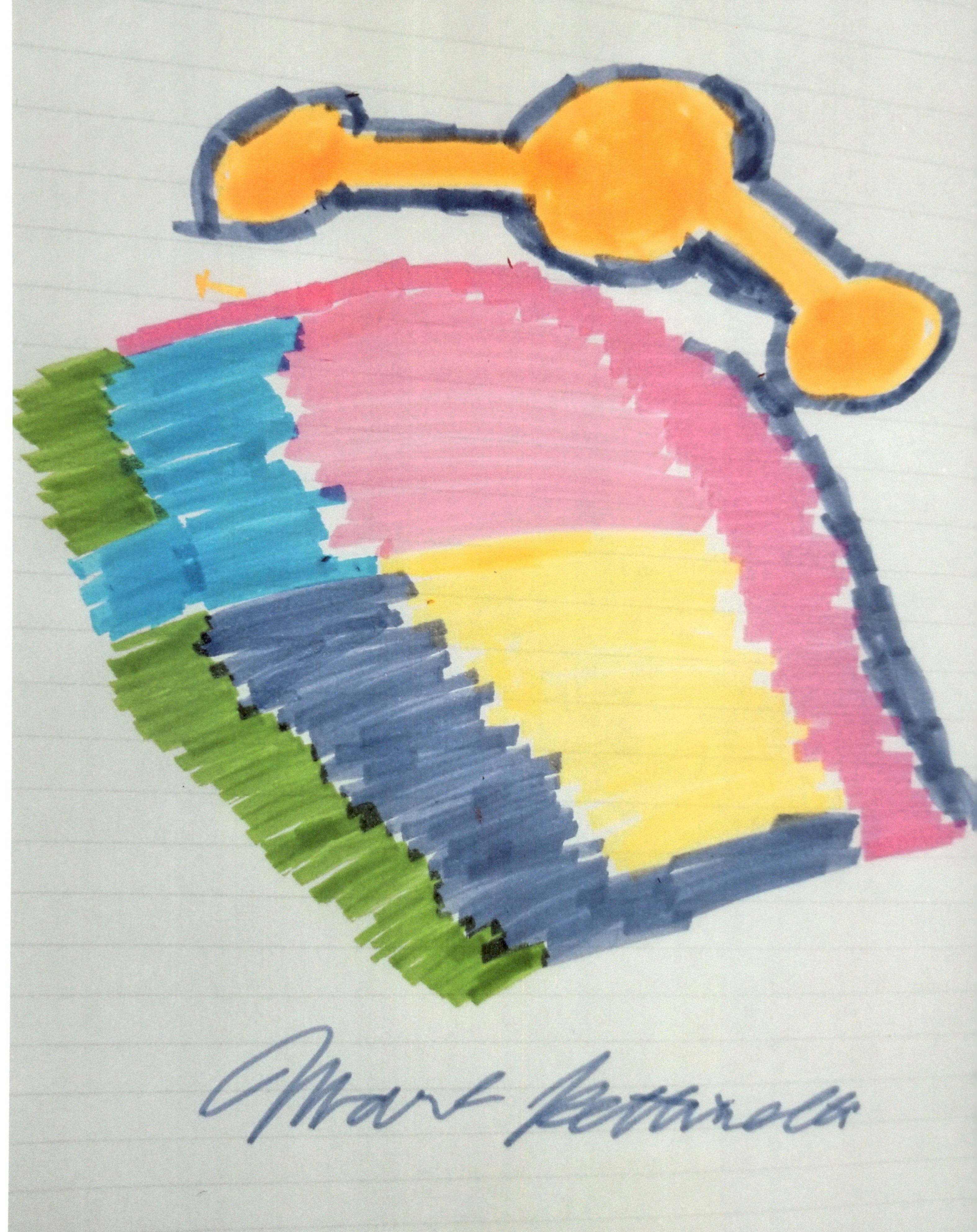

Mark Kostabi

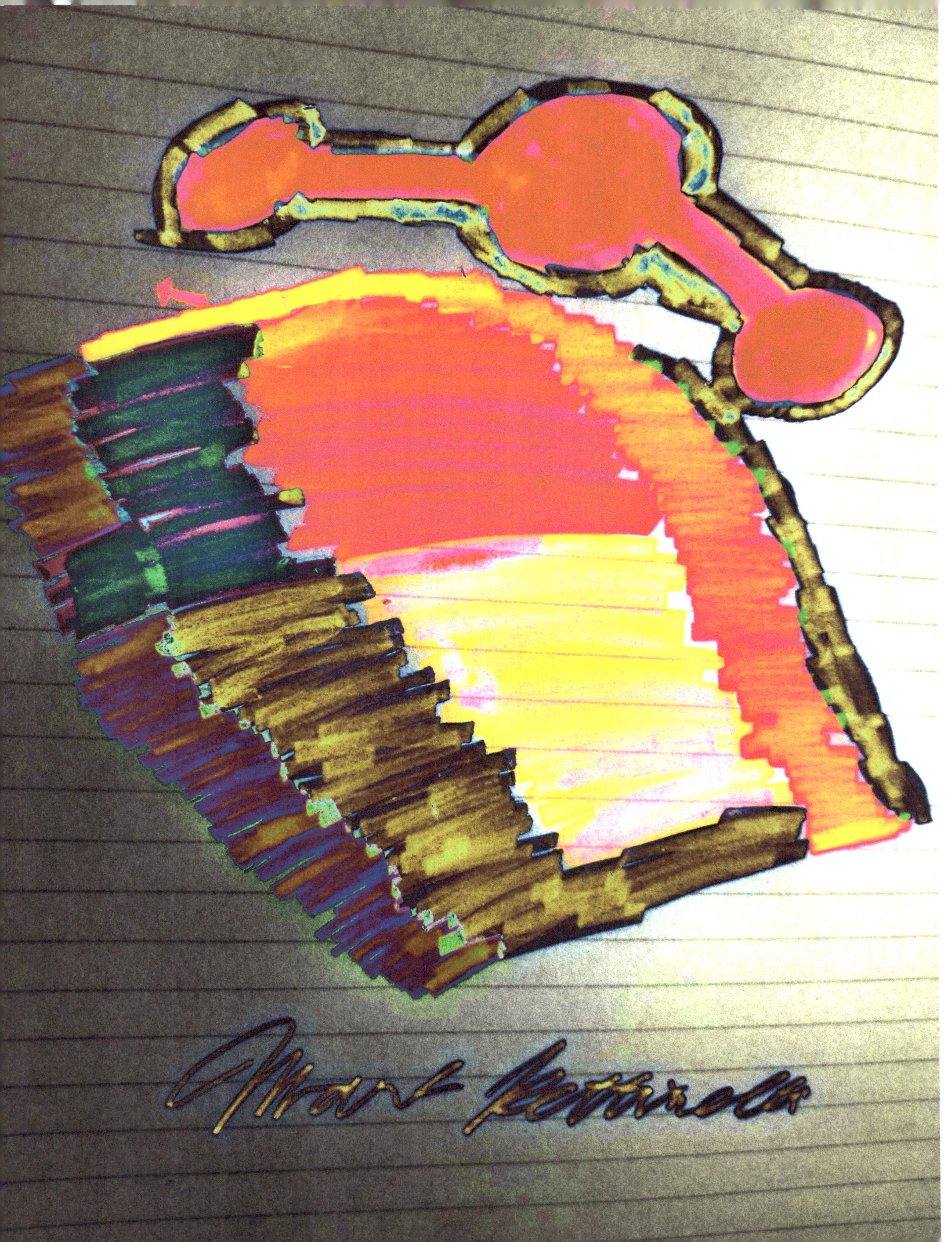

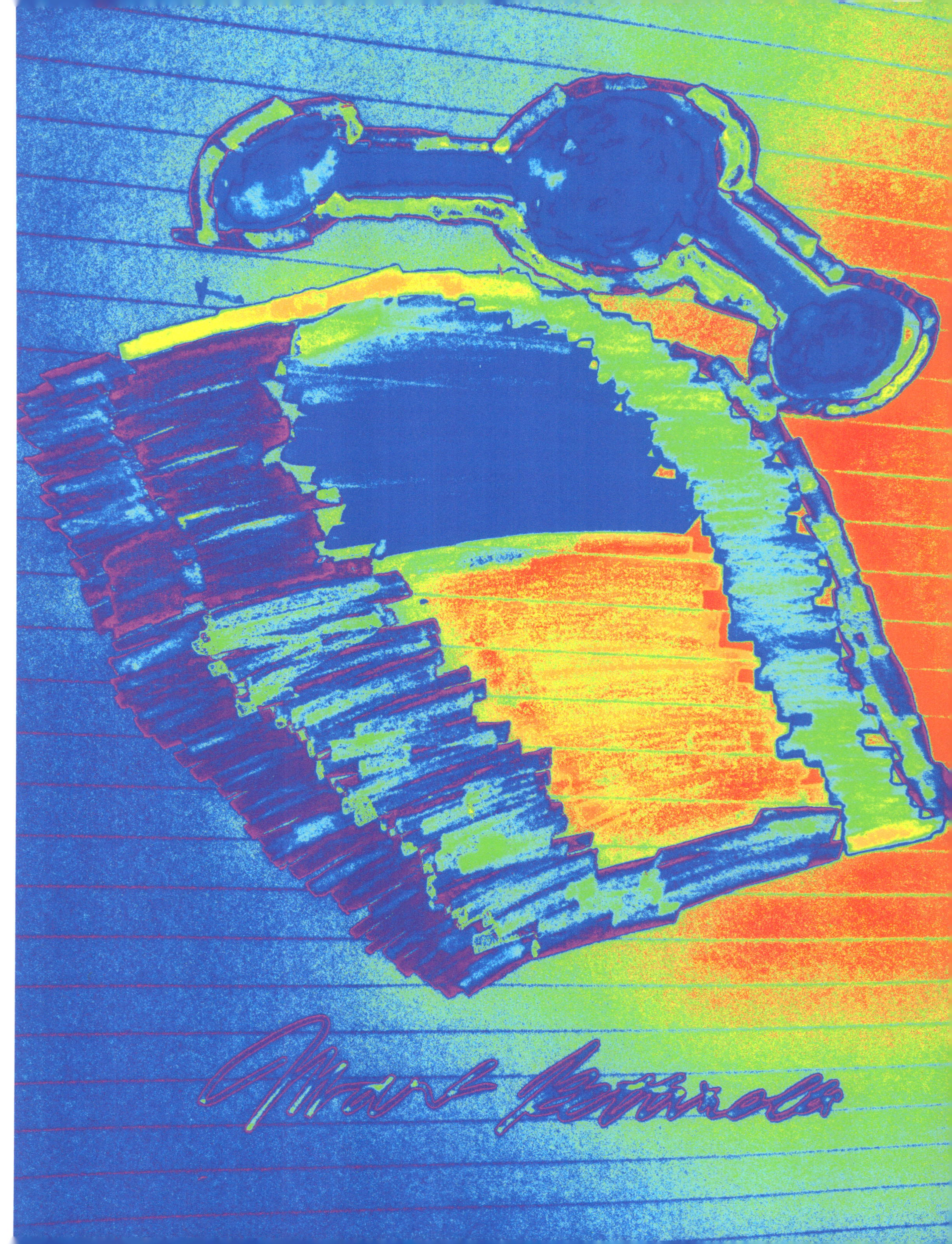

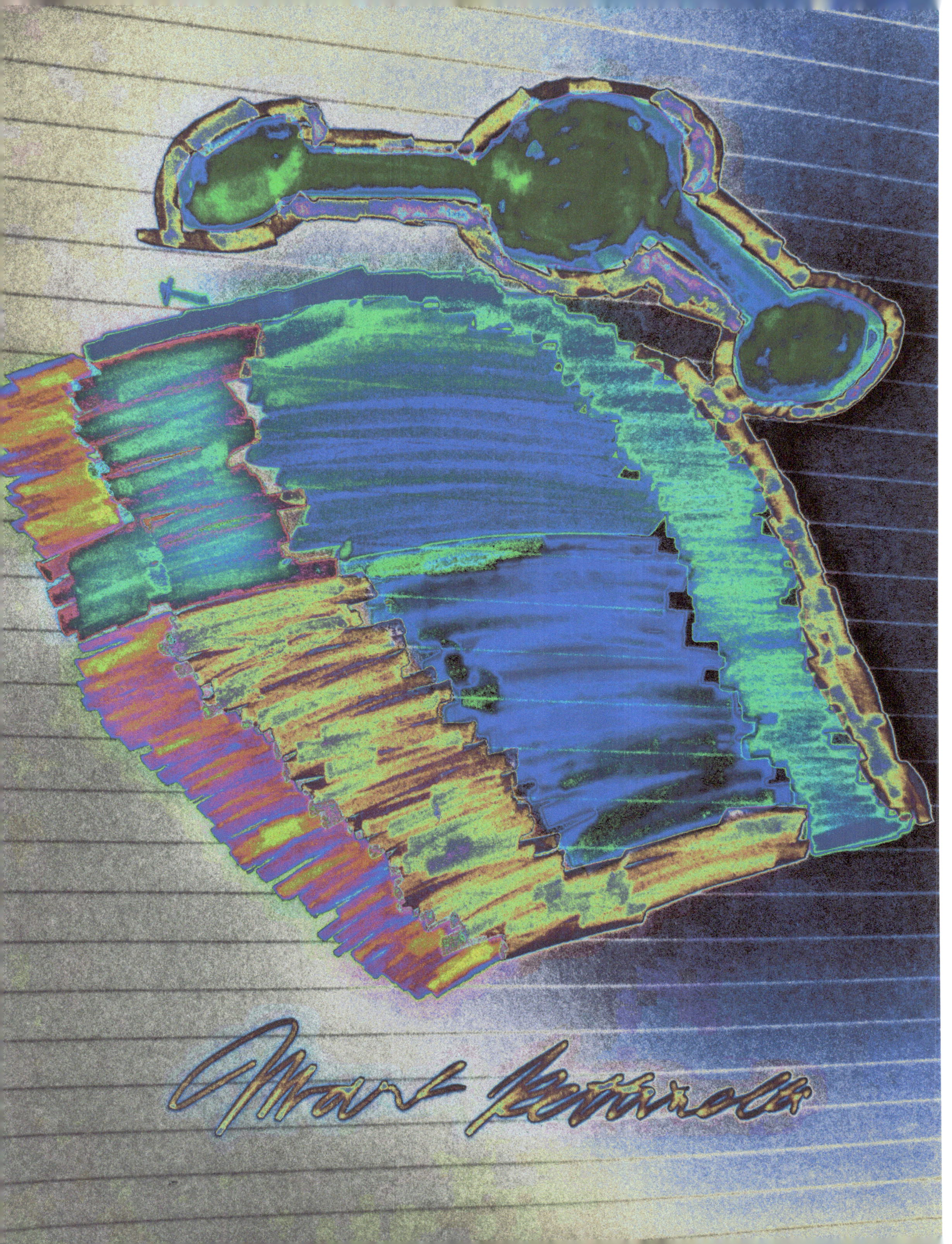

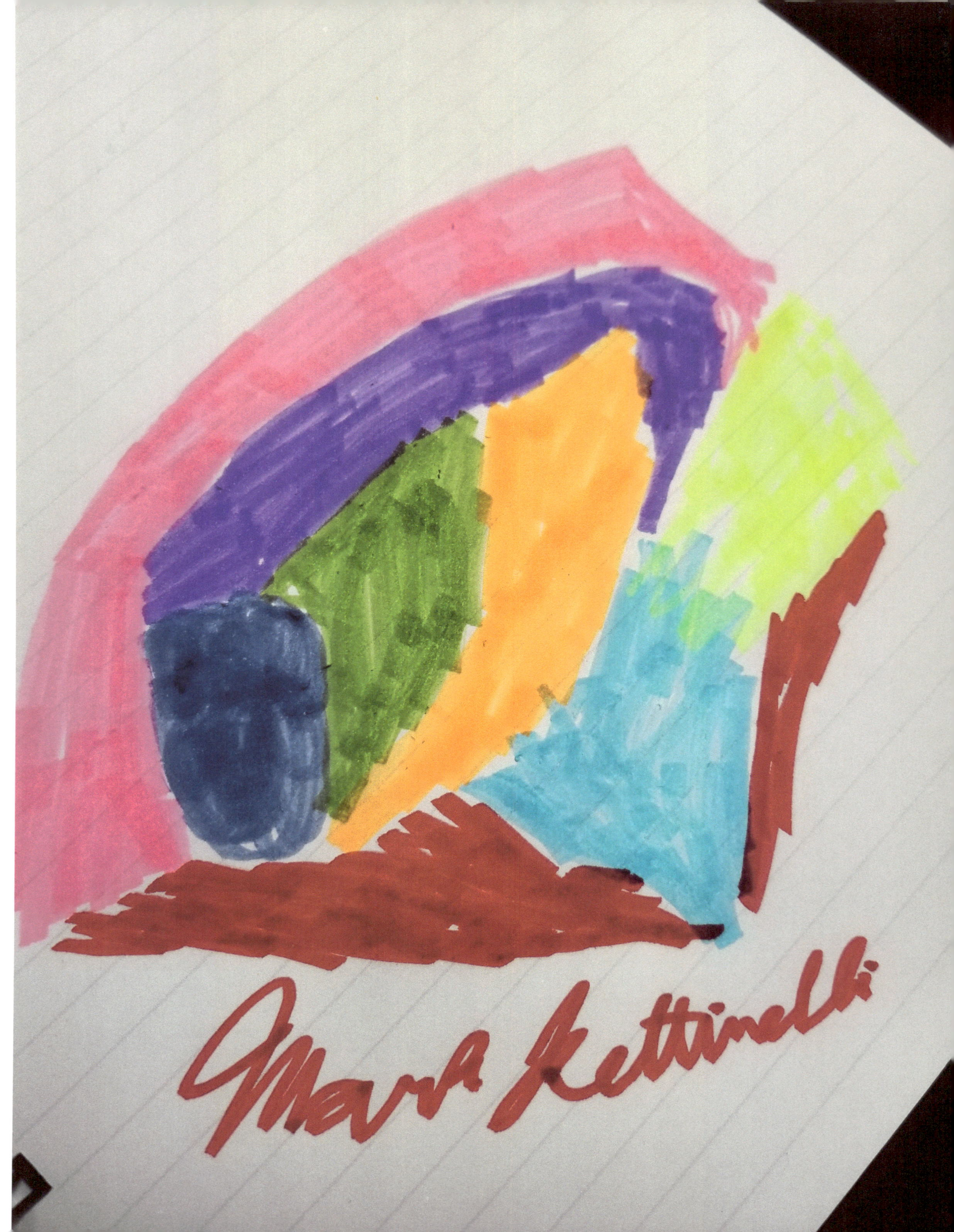

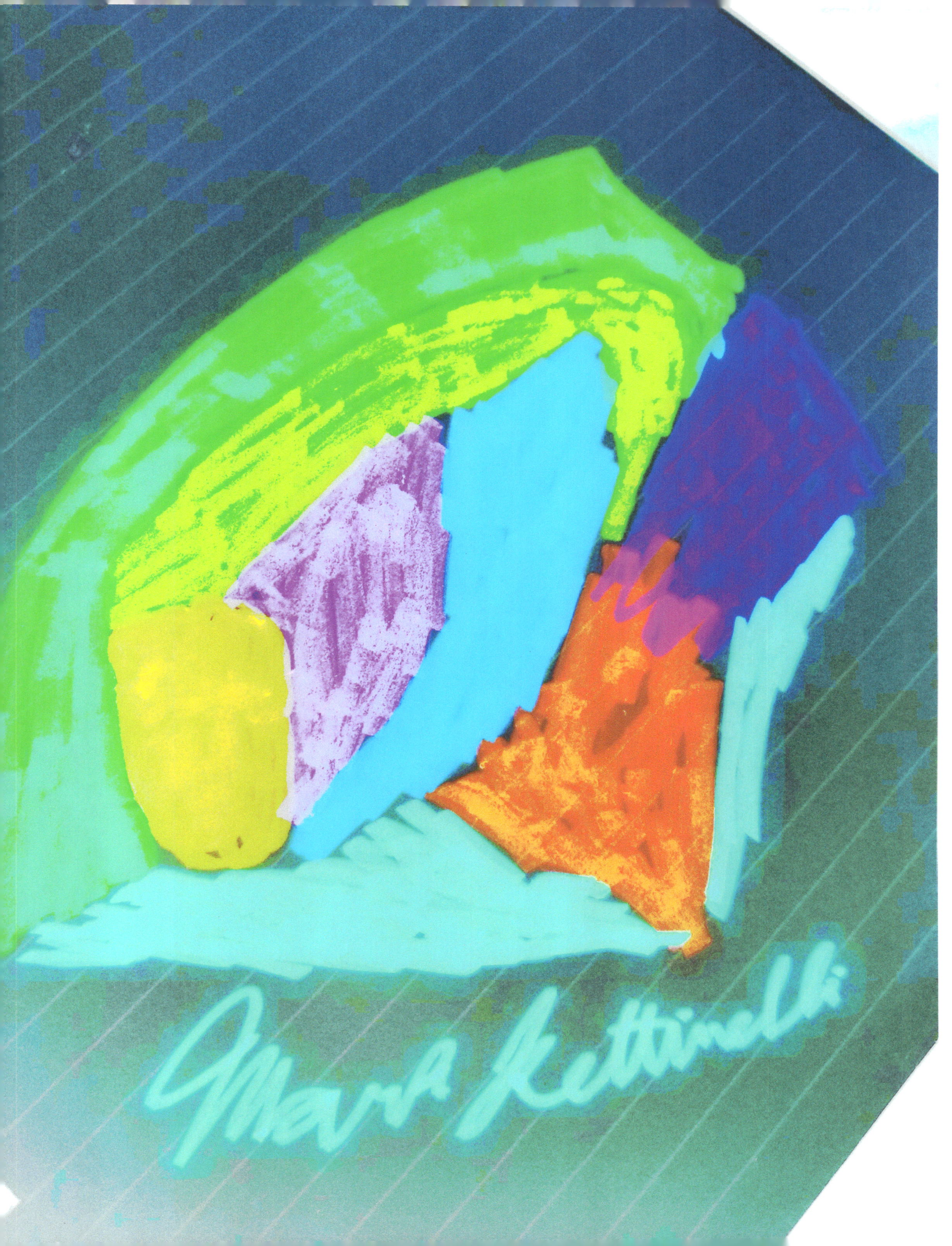

Mark Kettinelli

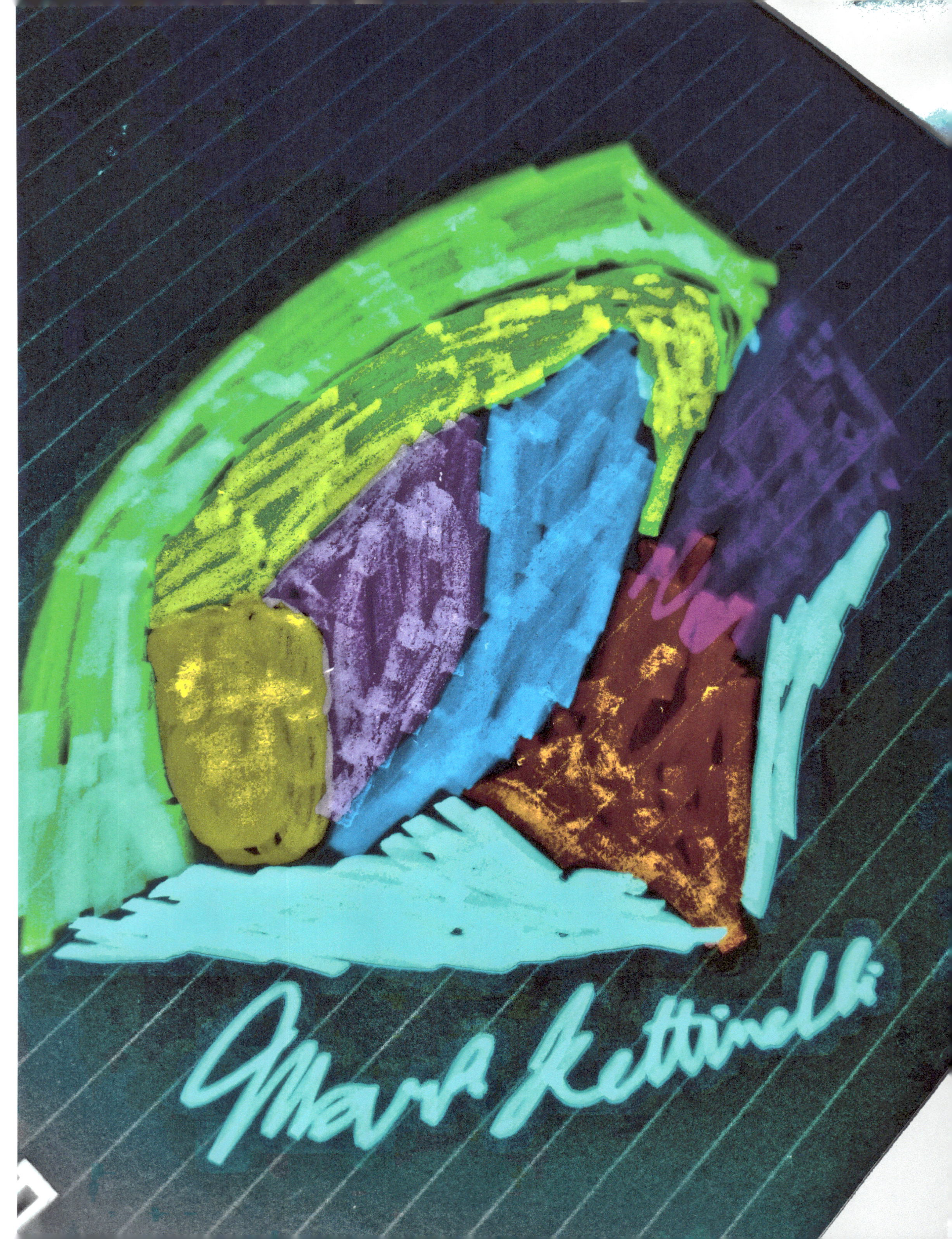

Mark Rettinelli